Printed in the United States of America

First Printing, 2018

ISBN 978-1-7326742-1-9

Aset Rising Publishing, LLC

www.asetrising.com

Instructions Not Given:
Building the Tribe

The Art of Co-Parenting & Blending Families

by Aset Rising & OB3

To our legacy, our children.

May our family make a mark on this world
that can never be erased.

Shout Outs!

Whew! This has been a journey! We want to make a special shout out to our children, Taylor, OB4, Demetrius, Nicco, Carmela, Madison, Roi, and the promise we made to one another over 20 years ago to be the best parents we could be. Although we have fallen short, you all have continued to be our priority and focus. We hope that each of you will grow up to see, even though we are human, and have fucked up often, we loved each of you FIERCELY. We loved you enough to get over our shitty marriage and work together to be your loving and dedicated parents. And then we wrote all about it in this kickass book.

Thank you for picking us.

- *Mom and Dad*

Preface

This is not your average co-parenting book if there is such a thing. This is a graphic story about two people who grew through loving, having children, marrying and divorcing one another to successfully co-parent our children. We use adult language and profanity as we share our personal story and touch on topics that are not easy to discuss.

We were never given any instructions on how to do this co-parenting and blending families thing. We are doing it by the seat of our pants trying to keep it together for the children. Hence the title, *Instructions Not Included: Building the Tribe*. We made many mistakes along the way and sometimes we still don't get it right. For instance, as Dub is co-authoring this book, she has not been able to successfully co-parent with her second husband, affectionately called #2 throughout the book. (Note: We are telling this story as transparently as possible without including the personal business of too many people.)

Make no mistake, we bring a lot of humor and realness to this difficult topic as we consider some of our choices and actions in hindsight. We are committed to our journey together as the parents of our children. But co-parenting is not and never has been easy. It requires two people to show up for the children despite everything else. The ego may tell you that it is OK to be difficult. Your circle of family and friends might even urge you to be difficult.

"Fuck him, girl. Make him pay. File child support!"

"Fuck it, if she won't let you be a dad then let her do it on her own."

This is what the peanut gallery will say. Silence them. Do what is best for your children. If that means you dead the ego and co-parent with your ex, do what you have to do. If it means you have to fight to the death to keep your children in a mentally and physically safe environment - fight! But remember: it's best you don't attempt to color your children's view of their other parent. There is nothing right about turning a child against his or her father or mother and we will never support or advocate that. Parental alienation is illegal and immoral. Let your child see the other parent for themselves and you keep doing your best for them.

Rest assured, Dub is actively working through the issues with her ex-husband, #2. In the meantime, she writes from a place of duality, as a mom who has a great co-parenting relationship with OB3 and an estranged relationship with #2. This duality lends a very honest point-of-view to the unique challenges co-parenting and blending families present. Dub's prayer is to one day be able to effectively co-parent and properly blend families with #2 for the sake of their daughters. Again, it takes two willing parties to successfully co-parent and your children deserve nothing less.

Let's get started.

Foreword

Greetings & Salutations,

Let me first commend you for making your family a priority and second for having the foresight to choose this work as a resource for your family. The concept of parenting without instructions is not new, but this installment into the lexicon of parenting literature is refreshing in that it reads very much like the conversation one would have with a wise, old and uninhibited grandparent, respectively.

This is especially the case as my experience of this family comes from co-author Aset Rising who I initially met during the developmental years of middle school. However, it was not until years later when I was invited to serve as part of the support system that would assist in her transition through the stages of her now concluded marriage to her second husband that I really came to know her. In that time, I found that the desire to become truly self-actualized is a constant goal of hers. In doing so, becoming the woman that would walk in her own greatness as a Spouse, Mother, Friend and Human is an inevitability. Those traits are merely a reflection of the entire family unit and the commitment to making their family one family versus several overlapping families. That commitment to being one is why you and your family can only be strengthened through the struggles of this representation of many modern-day families.

Now, I am not perfect but I am a licensed professional. Throughout my years in the helping profession, it has been my charge to assist children, adults, couples and families to identify their struggles. Whether it be anger, depression, anxiety, grief, guilt, distrust, goal-setting or something else, my goal is to aid individuals in utilizing the tools necessary to change their mindset and their situation. All of which is applicable to being part of a blended family. Speaking as a parent it is necessary to have someone in your world speaking to you as transparently, though raw, as what you will find in these pages. In either capacity, I am confident that Instructions Not Given: Building the Tribe gives you that! Enjoy. Learn. Apply!

Sabastan Moore, M.A., LPC
Progress to Purpose Concierge Therapy
www.progress2purpose.com

Chapter One:
Intro

Dub's Introduction

I am assuming you are reading this book for two reasons. One, you have a child or children. Two, you are no longer in a committed relationship with the mother or father of the child or children. Just take a deep breath. It is OK. Co-parenting is not as bad as the world has made it seem. It takes dedication, maturity, focus, compassion, understanding and forgiveness. But I am getting ahead of myself. I am Mom. That's my most common name. I am also called Dub, Kendra, Eva, Aset, and *That Bitch*. But, it's not what they call you it's what you answer to and I answer to "Mom" A LOT! I have five beautifully complicated children with two different men. Don't judge me! Even Jesus' mama had two baby daddies.

I was born to a teenage mother within a tight-knit family in Sunnyside, Houston, Texas. I came into this world fighting. Born premature, I required extra care and attention. My young mother allowed my great aunt and uncle to take on the majority of parenting duties when I was less than a year old. As the story goes, Meme and Ernie were in their sixties when I was in diapers. Being raised by elders made me an old soul. I listened to gospel music, spent weekends at church, and I thought peppermint candy was the best treat on the planet. I was showered with love and affection from everybody in the family except my Uncle Ernie. He was my favorite human but he was not affectionate. Hugs were sparse and kisses were non-existent.

I was a physically awkward kid because I was so lanky. Boys didn't flock to me even though I was funny, super smart, loyal and low-maintenance. I went from being the ugly duckling to becoming a blossoming swan over the summer of 1994. That's the summer I met with OB3 on a party line and we hooked up. OB3, my boyfriend and soon-to-be baby daddy, was a bad boy. He was a rebellious, exciting, fun, disappointing, cheating bad boy! I couldn't love that man more if they gave me two hearts. We met and he took me from my good girl shell to his ride or die chick. He turned out to be my second favorite human. I gave birth to our first child when I was eighteen years old. But I'll tell you all about how we met and fell in love in Chapter One.

For now, just know you have my mother to thank that we're telling this story at all. She told me I'd have to accept my failures with OB3 after our divorce and develop a friendship for the sake of our children. We did, and as the months turned into years, we interacted with many different parents, friends, acquaintances and family members who told us time and time again, *"Y'all need to write a book!"*

We would laugh and joke about touring the world transforming parents from baby mamas and baby daddies into co-parents by equipping them with the tools they would need to get it together for the children. Finally, our jokes have become a reality. We hope this book helps to move you one step closer to giving your children the best life possible complete with both parents.

As you read, keep in mind there are three sides to every story. My story, his story and the truth. This book is a melodious, honest version of our individual stories and our journey to the truth of co-parenting and blending our families.

Welcome! Fasten your seatbelt because this is going to be quite the ride.

OB3's Introduction

I have said this before and I will say it again so be warned. *I did not want kids.* I especially did not want as many kids as I ended up with. I asked my mom for a vasectomy on my 18th birthday. It doesn't take a genius to tell that her answer was no. Welcome to my world people! I am OB3. I had a good family, my grandmother and grandfather did the best they could with me, but the streets of Third Ward, Houston, Texas raised me. I was the baby son of my mom and dad. My dad was an addict and my mom was absent. My sisters spent all their time chasing men and my big brother was a dope dealer. My childhood best friend is in jail for life after being charged with killing a man in MacGregor Park for his watch. I have seen and done things that men my age may never experience and it has shaped me into the man and father I am today. I had so many plans for my chaotic life and fatherhood wasn't one of them.

Dub and I began dating at a young age. She was still in high school and I was fresh out of school. To be honest, she was one of many. But it didn't take long for things to become serious. Two and a half years into dating, our first daughter was born and my life, as I knew it, changed. Our daughter awakened a fire in my belly to be the best man I could be. The pressure I put on myself after her birth caused me to make many mistakes. Retrospect is 20/20. I'm hoping my honesty will prevent you from making the same mistakes I did.

I have been told time and time again that our story was like a soap opera and we needed to write a book. But it never seemed like a soap opera to me, it was our life. We were trying to figure out how to love but hate one another, while raising children who would become better than us. I'm proud to say I am a much better father now than when I started this fathering thing almost 21 years ago. Our biggest achievement is the way Dub and I have figured out how to co-parent and blend these families. *We did that*. I hope you enjoy a glimpse into our world as you read this. We are not professionals by any stretch of the imagination. We had no instructions. We made our own.

Chapter Two:
Dating - *First comes love*

Dub's Story

Boys were a new fascination of mine in my high school years. I had made it through middle school as 'the friend.' I would counsel my female and male friends through breakups, first dates, introductions, song choices, outfit changes, and anything boy/girl-related. I would just close my eyes and pretend that the guy was trying to impress me and my expert advice would flow like a river. My best friend, who is also my cousin, was a few years older than me. It was an advantage because I got to hang with her older friends and listen to all of the grownup gossip. She went to one of the most popular high schools in the city, Jack Yates Senior High, and I wanted to attend with her so badly it hurt. I begged my mom throughout my entire eighth grade year to let me go to Yates, a black school. I needed it. I required it. Attending predominantly white elementary and middle schools, on top of living with 70 year-old adults and spending weekends at church, left me with a huge social deficiency. I just had to go to Yates High School or so I thought! My mother didn't go for it. So, I settled on making as many friends as I could at the school I would be attending, so that I would not be so nervous on the first day of school.

My cousin, who went to Yates High School, along with her best friend and I would talk on the phone for hours about this guy or that guy. One particular guy attended my cousin's best friend church. His name was OB3. Apparently he was the new hype on campus since he had lost a lot of weight and changed up his wardrobe. I listened to the girls chatter incessantly about this guy for hours and felt like I knew him personally. A few parties at Stadium Bowl and St. Peters, and OB3's presence was short and brief. I don't think I actually saw his face the first two times we were at the same party. He was surrounded by a crowd of people. Girls and boys laughing and smiling at him like he was a celebrity. He had a charismatic personality that made you want to get closer to hear what he had to say, what he thought was cool, how he put a spin on the latest dance moves. Our first real introduction was over the phone. I do not recall the details of how we ended up on the phone together. I just remember one day a simple call from my cousin/best friend turned into a party line with OB3, Tasha, Maryssa, Dina, and T Mac. The conversation was lively. OB3 was the prominent voice, the jester, the guy that had all the right things to say. I fell silent on the call because I didn't want to sound lame. I was the youngest and goofiest of the group. I didn't want to stick out like a sore thumb.

Months later, all of a sudden I had a social life and it was popping. I'd become class president, joined the cheer squad and step team. I was also part of a service organization called

Majestic Ladies. I had parties to go to, games to cheer, pep rallies to attend, step shows to step in. Life was everything a teenage girl like me could ever want and much improved from spending the weekends at church with old people. Except I didn't have a boyfriend who went to my high school.

Winky Bear! I met Jason, AKA Winky Bear, on the school bus in Autumn 1994. He went to a neighboring high school, but we shared a school bus because we were part of a small group of black kids being bussed from the hood to magnet schools. He was a good guy, loved music, worked at the cool movie spot AMC Meyer Park 16 and he was my first. I remember how sweet, kind and gentle he was. The exact opposite of OB. Most of our times were spent on the school bus or on a movie date on the weekends. He was cool, but I was moving faster than I was thinking and wanted to date other guys.

OB3 and I talked on the phone sporadically at first. He would call every day for a week and then disappear for two weeks. I hated that about him. He was so inconsistent. I never knew what he was thinking or how he felt. I just had to wait until he picked me up off the shelf to play with me. One time, I decided to get his attention and told him that I was no longer a virgin. This definitely peaked his interest. I was not just the school church girl to him anymore. We talked a bit more frequently but we were nowhere near being in a relationship with each other.

He picked me up from step practice one day and took me to his house. His grandparents were not home so we had the house to ourselves. I recall turning down his street and the houses that were so big as we passed by. I recall the red seats in his car. Vivid bright blood red seats that were soft and velvety to the touch. The smell of his grandparents' home was very much like my own. We were both living with elderly people that was a connection that we would always share. His bedroom looked like an adult lived there. It had a Queen sized bed with marble headboard, side table, and dresser with a mirror. I had to look around twice to make sure we were in the correct bedroom. This dude was living large.

He smelled like soap, crisp clean Lever 3000 soap. It was a simple yet intoxicating smell. On the drive to his house he was very talkative. Full of conversation and stories about his day. In the bedroom, he had very little to say. He knew what he wanted and why he was there and he went straight to business. His assertiveness was a shock to my system, this little church girl was shocked. It was good. No it was great. No it was amazing! I was immediately hooked. He was my drug and I constantly needed a fix. I turned into a lying cheating dick feign. Every chance I got, regardless of where or how, I was going to get my fix. A relationship title did not bother me initially. It was just that good.

Eventually, after catching him with a few girls here and there, I wanted to be more than just a piece of meat. I had to put the cookie in the jar. That was the hardest thing I had to do up to that point in my life. I had to voluntarily go into dick rehab, dickmatization is real and dick is a helluva drug. The best thing that came from this was that we became really good friends during this period of abstinence. Not surprisingly, he didn't even notice the dry spell, probably too busy getting it from other girls. This battle was mine alone. I'd pretend to be busy so I didn't have time to see him. I knew I didn't have the willpower to resist him when in his presence. Yet, we talked every night about nothing important. Television, food, friends, future plans, school. OB3, although he was this cool kid that everybody wanted to be around, had this quiet vulnerability that he let me see. He was soft, not loud and boisterous. I enjoyed him as a friend but I wanted to be his girlfriend. Catching that title from him was much harder than I expected. He preferred a friends with benefits situation. I had to close my legs and demand dates before he even remotely took me seriously. We went to see Friday in the theaters and ate at Joe's Crabshack for dinner and that night a couple was formed. It was quite a ride from that day forward.

OB3's Story

That goddamn T Mac and fucking three-way. We stayed on the phone with some little girls daily. And I kept hearing this one name every day, *Dub*. I had to know who she was. T Mac talked about her too much so me being me I had to see. Friday night St. Peter's it is going down. T Mac hooked it up so we could meet face to face. We had been doing the phone thing for a couple of weeks so now it was time. I'm dancing (Yes, I am a dancer) when this group of girls started to watch. Oh I had to clown, DJ Aggravated made it easy for me. I didn't know she was one of the girls in the group. Introductions were made and that's where it all started with T Mac, Fucking Three-way and St. Peters.

We started out as just friends, telephone buddies type shit. She was my nerd friend and didn't have too many of those. I really didn't know how to have a girl as a friend for real. I really wanted to get in her pants. Let's be real. I was a pure dog. Looking to plant my flag. I can't lie and say I saw something special or any corny shit like that. I didn't want to commit to what I was wearing the next day let alone a girl. I had a few young ladies on my team back then. Now I had a brain on my team. Yep that's how I viewed Dub then as the Brain. I had other chicks to show off on the block but never had one that could write a paper for me, so OK this was new.

We went back and forth for a while. Me being a pure asshole and her being the hopeless romantic trying to change my ways. Somehow we ended up as a couple. And so our story begins.

Chapter Three:
Kids - *Then comes the baby in the baby carriage*

Dub's Story

I was never supposed to have children. My life plan in high school included a pair of cocker spaniels and a live ass condo in downtown Houston. I was supposed to go to college at FAMU, and enjoy the full experience and the richness of a HBCU. I wanted to be in a sorority and travel around the world in my twenties before I settled down and got married in my thirties. My early life was mapped out or so I thought. Three things changed the course of my life forever. First, my mother fell ill. Second, I was not allowed to go on my senior trip with my friends to Europe. Third, I watched my boyfriend become a father. Follow this story in reverse with me.

———————————————

It was a hot and sticky August afternoon and we were driving around in the Taurus in silence. The heat was so thick you could cut it with a knife, and the tension inside the car was thicker. My boyfriend, the guy that I was passionately and madly in love with, the guy I would give my last dollar and breath for, the guy that I thought was my best friend, that guy just told me that he had a newborn son that was born the day before. He tried to be empathetic towards me but he was so proud to be the father of his first son that he really couldn't hide his joy from me. Joy was not the emotion I could relate to in this moment. Red. That is what I felt. I don't know what emotion to attach that to, all I know is I felt, saw and thought in RED. How do you respond to this type of news?

"Congratulations?"

"I am so happy for you?"

"It's a boy, that's what's up?"

My best response was silence and I just let the words hang in the air. B was talking to me about how the hook up with the chick was just a one time thing, blah blah blah but I heard nothing. All I wanted to do was get out of that car and far away from him.

Less than eight weeks before he told me about his newborn son, I had my first abortion. I was going into my senior year in high school and he didn't want children. He was very adamant about that. I hid it from my mom and my best friends. No one knew about this but the two of us. I remember how attentive he was to me during that time. He was there with my medications

14

and a super size bag of skittles. He wiped away my tears, he told me it was all going to be OK, and maybe we would have a child one day. He was doing all of this while he was fully aware that another woman was calling him the baby daddy.

Dirty son of a bitch! I was so mad. Nah fuck that I was hurt. Deeply. My tears were hot as steam as they fell from my eyes in that car driving down Scott St. Every single time I got comfortable in this relationship he would crack another piece of my heart. *"Why am I still here?"* was a question I asked myself every few months. I took the news in silence. I grieved in silence. I moved on in silence. When I finally spoke, I had one question. *"Do you want to be with her?"* He swore on everything that he loved that he did not. My next response was shocking, *"Then we can raise this baby together, if that is what you want."*

I watched him become a dad and he was a good dad too. He would jump whenever his baby mama called. B would keep Shorty with him and take him to college classes with him. He would talk to Shorty with such wisdom. The baby was less than six months and he would read the dictionary to him. I know that sounds silly but B really did grow up in front of me. I was so proud and extremely hurt at the same time. I fell in love with Shorty though. He was the center of my world whenever he was around. His smile was infectious. His cheeks were so kissable. His skin was chocolate brown, his hair was dark and curly. I could not help but fall in love with him. He was such a happy baby. He was an innocent baby. He had nothing to do with his parents' decision to break my heart.

My relationship with the baby mama was fucked up. I took every opportunity I could find to make her jealous. We played this back and forth game all the time. I was young and dumb and full of cum. I didn't see B as the problem. No, that bitch was the issue and she was going to feel me. I showed up to her job just so she would be responsible for making my food but I would not acknowledge who she was, at all. I would pretend to butt dial her phone so she could hear the three of us playing happy family with her baby on the weekends we had him. This was before the social media era, so you had to be real about your mess and do it face to face. I would drive down her street to see if he was there with her while I was babysitting the baby. If she would page B (yes this was the era of pagers and two-ways), I would intercept it and delete the message if it didn't have anything to do with the baby. I wanted to hate her, she gave him his first son, and they were a family and I was just the outsider. I wanted to hate her but I could not. Her son had my heart and I couldn't hate her and love him. So it settled into a mild dislike as I learned to pretend she never existed. The ability to make her disappear in my world is a skill I have used many times later in life but we'll get to that later.

We worked our schedule around him all of the time and the more he as the baby got older, I suggested that we put the baby in part-time daycare nearby so that I could still go to school and he could work. We settled on a perfect place nearby and went to sign him up.

"OK, the paperwork looks good. We just need the baby's birth certificate, immunization record and we are all set." The worker at front desk informed.

I turned to B, fully expecting him to have these documents.

"I don't have it. His mom said I don't need them." He said with embarrassment in his voice.

"Ma'am we will back in a few days." I had to clean it up and get him out of there before I could react.

At this age, I did not walk away from challenges. I always looked for a way to get exactly what I wanted. Instead of going through his mom, we went to DHPS office to get the birth certificate. Guess the fuck what!?!?!?! He couldn't get a copy of it because there was another's man named listed on the birth certificate. I gasped as the clerk said the words. B looked at me at least five times before he could register it. He confronted his baby mama over the phone and she pulled the only card she had. She stopped letting us see Shorty. B tried to hide his feelings about it but he was hurt. Actually, I think he was devastated in a way no man should have to feel when it comes to a child. He had poured so much into Shorty. His name was tattooed on his chest! Now it was a possibility that it was not his kid. I watched with my own eyes as he shut down his feelings about the baby. He went into protection mode and removed all of his clothes, shoes, toys, and pictures from our home. It hurt him too much to see reminders everywhere. Adding insult to injury, his family decided to side with the baby mama. They tried to persuade him to not pursue paternity and to let things stay the same.

"B, you know I didn't raise you like this!" Grandma Millie chided him.

"Grandma, if he is not mine then he should not carry my name and you should accept that." B pleaded with her trying to get her to understand.

"That girl says it is yours, so it is yours."

"This not the old days, it don't work like that. I can find out and that is what I plan to do. I can't believe you don't have my back on this one. You barely know this girl!" B yelled as he walked out the door.

He did the only thing he thought he could do as a young black man with no legal representation. He went to the attorney general to file child support on himself so he could establish paternity and visitation. On the day of the paternity test, I woke up with pain deep in my heart. I just didn't want to know anymore. I wanted it to be OK, I wanted it to just to be a coincidence, and I wanted him to be our son. However, B had fire in his belly now. He demanded answers and there was no turning back. We sat in the lab waiting for him to be called to take the test. I was very pregnant with our second child, OB4, and I sat across from his baby mama and kept looking in her eyes. I felt like if it was true, I would see it in her eyes. All I saw was defiance, no fear. Just a plain *"fuck you."* So I looked away.

Weeks later the paternity results came in the mail. OB3 was not home, he was in the streets hitting licks. This was a huge surprise, we did not expect the results to return so quickly. I held the mail in my hand like it weighed of stone. I did not know if I should call him or wait until he got home. I left it on the couch for a few hours before I decided to call him and tell him it was there. He was home within minutes.

He opened the letter, read it and let it drop to the ground. There was a ZERO percent chance that he was the father.

"B. B, talk to me. What are you thinking?"

"I am thinking I want to whoop that ho ass!"

"Nah B. No violence. You promised."

"What am I supposed to do? She played me like a fucking fool for years and that ain't my baby! What am I supposed to do to make this OK?"

"I don't know. Just come sit down with me and let's figure this out."

"Nah, I'll be back. I promise, I won't lay a finger on her but she will feel this pain."

What did he do? He went to the closest copier store and made 100 copies of the paternity test. He drove down the street where she lived street jamming DJ Screw and tossed the paternity test copies all over the street. Neighbors came outside to watch the debacle. If I am not mistaken her family was outside when he did this. He totally and completely embarrassed the fuck out of that girl and child. It was so embarrassing that her family called his family to tell on him. It was absolutely true OB3 style. He never really had to put his hands on you or raise your voice to let you know how he felt. He had shamed the fuck out of the girl as I sat on the couch feeling bad for her. I prayed for her, but mostly I prayed for Shorty. He was no longer my baby anymore, my Lil Chunky. I could not imagine what she was feeling but I knew that she was a human and it hurt. I also knew that I could not pray for them in B's presence so I had to do it at that moment alone. I prayed for her and our baby which was now just her baby. When B is mad at you, you are dead to him. I knew we would never see that baby again. I was right. Shorty was eighteen years old before I saw him again. He passed me in a store and I instantly knew who he was and wanted to reach out to him. He had no recognition of me in his eyes. I never existed.

I found the ex-baby mama on Facebook many years later and apologized to her for being a young stupid bitch. I learned so much from that experience. I learned that I could be a good mom and B could be a great dad. I learned that being messy was not me. I learned that I should have left B if I was so hurt, or stay and forgive totally without holding grudges. Lessons learned.

———————————————

In Spring Break of '97 and I was supposed to be in Europe with my best friends. This was planned for at least a year. Every year our history teacher made the trip and that was the only trip I talked heading into our senior year of high school. I worked part time in senior year but not nearly as much as I needed to in order to fund an international trip across the pond. My mom, who was initially very excited for me and the trip, began to shy away when payments were required. She never said she did not have the money, she just never produced the money. It eventually became crystal clear that my mom was not going to be able to afford to send me away to Europe. In typical disrespectful teenage fashion, I lashed out and began breaking every rule.

During Spring Break, since I couldn't go to Europe I spent the week attached to the hip with OB3 and friends. We went out every single night and we had sex every single chance we could. Every single place we could. My mom, sick on the couch, had very little energy to deal with my silly ass tantrums. I would walk in at almost dawn some days and some days I would stay with B all night. I did not care at all. I did not feel bad at all. The week was over faster than I anticipated. My friends were back from Europe and my teenage rebellion melted away as life returned to normalcy. Except I was always tired and sick to my stomach. My mom took me to the doctor and they gave me fluids and pain medications because we thought it was the stomach flu. That did seem to help me for a few days. Then the fatigue returned again with a vengeance. I began to sleep in the corner of the classrooms at school. I missed classes often. I was barely passing my classes, something was wrong. This was not me.

As prom approached, I began picking up weight. All I had energy to do was eat. Sleep and eat. Finally it dawned on me. I was fucking pregnant. DAMN! I was going away to college this could not happen now. I had finally healed from the abortion heartbreak thanks to B's new baby. This could not happen now. I was on birth fucking control. This could not happen now. My mom is sick on the couch. This could not happen now. I am the golden child of my family, set to break the teen pregnancy curse. This could not happen now. I had to take a pregnancy test immediately. I left school and went straight the nearest pharmacy. I sat in the teacher's bathroom at school and peed on a stick. Within seconds, less than 30 seconds, the damn stick was positive. I believe in confirmation, so I took the second test. The second test was positive within seconds too. I am fucking pregnant. B just had a baby nine months earlier and I just knew he was going to be livid. My mom is going to be livid. How am I going to tell my best friend Alzay, he is going to be LIVID!!!! I decided not to tell anyone anything until I knew what I wanted to do. This was my decision and I had to think it through first. *"FUCCCCCCCCCCCCCK! Fuck!"* Those were the first words out of my mouth. My yell vibrated through the empty stalls.

I kept the news to myself for several weeks before I went to B with the news. He had recently been in a car accident and undergoing treatment for his injuries. I didn't want to make the situation any more complicated but I needed to talk it out with him before I could make a final decision.

As we were leaving his doctor appointment, I turned to him and said *"B, I have something important to tell you."*

"What's up lil mama? You been acting weird lately." He glanced over to me to check my body language. I was sitting as far away from him as possible. I was afraid that if I let him touch me I would lose the nerve to say what I was going to say.

"B, I know you said you didn't want a bunch of kids but..." I trailed off, losing my nerves.

"We gonna have a baby?" he asked. The tone in is voice was not what I expected. He seemed almost excited.

"Yea B. We gonna have a baby." I finally let slip from my lips.

"I hope it is a girl. Daddy's girl. I am going to buy her some pink shorts and shoes." He got lost in thought as he planned his relationship with his baby girl.

I sat there staring out of the window. Ironically, as he was happily discussing his baby girl we were driving past the abortion clinic that we went to at the beginning of this school year. Tears streaming down my face, I was happy that he wasn't asking me to have another abortion. I was confused at his sudden shift from less than a year ago but I didn't want to ruin his moment. I pushed the button on the seat to lean it back and I took a nap. This kid was zapping the life from me already. I had to summon the courage to tell my family and that was going to take everything in me, I needed to rest.

Less than seven months later we were the proud parents of a beautiful, purple-lipped, curly haired, perfectly brown-skinned baby girl, Taylor. She turned our lives completely upside down. Our relationship did not make it to the end of the pregnancy. I was heartbroken and still in love with him deeply but having the baby to fall in love made it easier to get through it. I learned from this experience that my heart could expand larger than ever imagined. I learned that a baby does not save a relationship. I learned so much from an unplanned pregnancy and becoming a mother. I learned that I have strength buried inside of me so deep that I could finish a college semester on bed rest with straight A's. I learned that there is no love like a love for your seed, life shifts when you learn you can give life.

Before I gave birth to a child and before B had an outside baby on me, I lost my instructions for womanhood. My once strong upbeat off-key soprano singing mother slowly went from having a cold to a sick and shut in shell of herself. She no longer could attend church or work. Her body began to shrink into her small frame. Our family would come and go all the time checking on her and leaving with sad eyes and heavy heart. After a while she stopped allowing people to see her because she was so small and frail. She stopped checking my grades. She stopped calling me out about missing curfew or not cleaning up behind myself. I went from being under the strict eye of Peanut to having free range to roam the city in her car without so much as one cuss word. The scariest part about all of this is I had absolutely no idea what was wrong with her. Like many families, my family was always shrouded in secrecy. We kept so many secrets that even our secrets had secrets. Needless to say, my mother was not the open, talkative type. She would just lay on the couch and watch Law and Order. She could not eat or cook or drive herself to appointments. She never complained or spoke of any pain or discomfort. You knew she was ill and you knew she was not giving up, she just needed the time to just be. Mama prayed to God all day and every night. Loudly, proudly, thanking Him. She would still bathe herself even though it took an hour. She still doted on my baby sister Ashley when she could and cussed her out when she needed the discipline. She was just weak. Tired. She would come into the bedroom with me and just lay there with me without talking. I did not know what to say so I just talked to her about whatever came to mind. My childhood, my dreams and all the things I wanted to do with my life. I asked her to explain to me why didn't I live with her as a kid and why she didn't take me with her after she had my sister and moved? So many answers came to me in those months that my mom would just lay in bed with me. We healed from all the years that we were apart from one another during those talks in my bed watching Lifetime TV.

One day out of the blue my cousin decided to tell me about my mother's diagnosis. At this point, I had already acted horribly during spring break, blamed her for missing Europe, overspent for prom and was pregnant but did not know how to tell her. I sat in the parking lot yelling at God. I was just getting to know her. I was just getting the chance to have her as a mom after almost 10 years of watching her live her life apart from me. We were just getting to the point where we had inside jokes. I didn't want to believe my cousin. So I went directly to my mom.

"Mama, the family is spreading horrible rumors about you!" I burst into the room screaming with tears still falling.

"What are they saying baby?" My mom asked as she weakly tried to pull herself up.

"They say you dying. You got AIDS and you dying." I sobbed.

"That is not a rumor baby. That is the truth. I am sorry you had to hear from somebody besides me." My mama said with her head hanging down.

"Why? Why didn't you tell me? Mama, why? What am I going to do without you?" The tears are not stopping and I am headed towards full panic attack.

"Baby, I didn't want you to be ashamed of me. I wanted you to remember the good times with me. I didn't want you living every day waiting for me to die. They told me I was going to die 4 months ago. I am still here." She said with tears falling from her eyes.

"Why would I be ashamed of you? Why would you not tell me and everybody knew! Four months, oh my God, Mamaaaaaaaaa!" I wailed and crawled across the floor to lay my head in her lap.

"Stop crying, you will upset the baby." She said.

My head shot up, *"The baby? How did you know about the baby?"*

"I am a mom. I know my daughter."

"I can't do this without you."

"You can and you will. I will be around for as long as I can fight. I have prepared you to live life without me. You didn't know

the lessons that were being taught but they were. You and that baby will be OK. Promise me you will remember your lessons."

"I promise."

A few hours later after I told B he came running to the house to be with my mom. Their relationship had evolved as we got older, they seemed to genuinely enjoy each other. Knowing what was wrong and seeing her made his heart feel so heavy.

He sat next to her feet and said, *"Hey beautiful, what can I do to help?"*

"I have just one request son, just take care of my child. Stick by her side and do not let her do this alone." She said as-matter-of-factly as possible.

"I can do that Ms. Peanut. I promise."

My mom fought for her life like a true warrior for almost 2 years after this conversation. My mother was there for me while I was on bedrest during my pregnancy and had to stop school. She wiped away my tears and told me that I would finish one day and not to worry. She was there for the birth of our daughter, the first grandbaby. I saw the tears fall from her eyes as she thanked me after holding her grandbaby for the first time. I watched her spoil her grandbaby Taylor every single day that she had the strength to do so. She fed her, dressed her, read to her, sang to her, every single chance she could. She would cry when the baby would cry. She would spend hours sitting in the rocking chair with the baby and talking to her quietly as I slept or caught up on homework.

———————————

Carmela Wyatt, aka Peanut, our mother, a sister, a daughter, a friend, a faithful child of God, died surrounded by my uncle James, myself, OB3, her granddaughter and her youngest daughter, Ashley in September 1998 after a thirteen year fight with HIV/AIDS.

———————————

I learned from this lesson that life is so short and so precious. I learned that OB3's loyalty to my family made me love him more as a family member than a romantic partner. I learned that my mom had amazing strength that she passed that strength down to me in lessons that I didn't know I was learning. I learned that life plans change and you have to go with the flow or stay stuck in the pain. I wish that my mother were here to meet our other children. I wish she was here to see how we have stayed together as a family no matter what happens, no matter what. Her promise was the greatest lesson.

Our next child was born almost 3 years after Taylor was born. I finally had my boy. OB3 finally had his namesake. I prayed for this child. I prayed over this child. I was so honored to carry a son because I knew that I would finally have a piece of OB3 all to myself that I didn't have to share with anyone else. He would love me like OB3 couldn't. He was going to be a mommy's boy and I didn't care what anyone had to say about it. I cherished my time alone with the baby in my belly. I fell so deeply in love with our son. Every kick, every movement was like an inside joke between Baby OB4 and myself. All the things that OB3 struggled with I vowed to keep away from my son. He would not hate women because his mom had abandoned him. No, I was going to be right there and he was going to love me. I was never going to leave him or mistreat him. My pregnancy became a high risk pregnancy that had me in the hospital for months. I was isolated because most of my family hated the fact that I was still with OB3. They didn't understand our dynamics. After 20 weeks of bed rest and an eventful birth our son was born. OB4 was less than 4 hours old when he flipped over for the first time in his incubator. I knew we were in for many surprises with this one. I did honor my promise to him in the womb. He was my baby, the love of my life. I clung on to him so tight and didn't want to share him with anyone, not even his dad. He has been to me exactly what I wanted him to be. All the good parts of OB3. I learned from my son what a mother's love could really feel like.

Our next set of children, we call them *The Twins*, were a product of two affairs. I am not sure if we should call them affairs because we were separated at the time for many years and in relationship with other people. Our son, Nicco, was born in January. Our daughter, Carmela, was born in April. It was not planned. I was already pregnant with a girl before OB3 ever told me about his pregnancy with a boy. As expected, people thought we were complete nuts when we got back together after having outside children. It actually restarted our relationship because we were finally even for the first time in a long time. I know that sounds mad crazy but it was so true. *The Twins* forced both of us to grow up. *The Twins* taught us that children can really change you as a person if you let them. One saved my life while the other gave me true meaning of unconditional love.

Carmela saved my life because before she was born, I had been in an 11 year on-again, off-again relationship with her dad, #2, as his mistress. Less than a year before she was born we had a nine and a half week affair during which he'd left his wife and we lived together. During that time we consummated the relationship and I was madly in love and addicted to him. Then one day he was gone. He went back to his wife and children with no warning or explanation. That was the scariest fight I've ever had with depression. I attempted suicide and almost succeeded twice. One day in Autumn of 2004, #2 popped up on my doorstep and said, "Let's have a baby." Without thought, I said yes and was pregnant within the month. Once I was pregnant, he left and told me to abort the baby. That's when OB stepped back in. He was worried I was going to go back to that very dark place, but I did not because this time I had a piece of #2 with me at all times, growing inside of me. All of my energy went towards my pregnancy and redeeming myself with OB3.

Nicco taught me unconditional love because from the moment OB3 told me he was having a baby with another woman I approached it differently than I did with Shorty and his mom. I was aware this was a direct result of OB3's decision and not the other woman. As soon as Nicco was born, I fell in love with him in a way that I'd never known. It was a decided love. A 'I choose you, little boy' type of love. His mother was diagnosed bipolar disorder, refused treatment and abused medication. She would make our lives so hard because she would let us see Nicco, but then snatch him away. Child Protective Services would become involved and he'd be with us until she'd get herself together again and then he would be gone for months, again. I would ache for him, I missed him as if my own child had been ripped from my arms. I tried SO hard to work with his mom. OB3 gave up trying, but I did not. I could not. I loved Nicco as God intended us to love, wholly, without limits, just because he existed.

OB3's Story

I would like to start by saying I DIDN'T WANT NO DAMN KIDS!

Thank you.

I'll admit I was not the best person in my teens and early twenties. I looked at life through a very small lens in those days. Anything beyond selling dope and smoking weed wasn't taken seriously. I lived life fast, no brakes, straight gas. But you know what? Life has a way of fucking up your flow.

Man, I remember that bullshit call in August of '96! I had a whole kid, a fucking newborn baby at *20-years-old*. Oh, I knew I'd fucked up this time. I told Dub about the kid thinking she was going to cuss me out, cry and all that shit. But no. She surprised me when she said, "We're going to take care of this baby," and kept it pushing. I thought she had lost her natural mind. I thought I could use her lapse in judgment and sanity to my advantage. My slick ass tried to keep both of my women happy but that didn't go as planned. I can't lie. I had fun turning the situation into a competition. I'd think to myself, '*Who's willing to do the most to keep OB3 happy?*' Then the ace under the sleeve was pulled.

On a ride down 610-West headed toward the Astrodome my life changed for the good...again. It was on that fateful ride that Dub told me I was about to be a daddy for the second time in only a year's time. I wanted to open that door and roll out onto the freeway.

"Oh hell no! Not again," I thought to myself. *"What the hell am I going to do now?"* I was trying to keep my cool, but my thoughts were racing.

Dub looked square at me and told me she was having this kid with or without me. The choice of whether I'd be involved was mine to make.

I took a deep breath and said, *"Fuck it, OK."*

Saying OK was the easy part. I had no job or car and was living at home. You know, the starter pack for the Father of the Year Award. Don't forget, I was a weed-smoking drug dealer at the time. So I did the only thing I knew how to do. I dove headfirst into the streets. Can you blame me? The streets were all I knew. I used them to escape my life. Real grown, little boy shit, I know. It's crazy to think I was putting my life in danger just to avoid facing it. The whole time Dub was pregnant my boys would talk about me having a son. But I didn't want a boy. I prayed for a daughter. I knew in my heart

I needed a person in my life that would force a change in me. I felt a son would make things worse for me. Dub wanted a boy, her own little version of OB3. If our first born was a boy he would have been doomed. I would have molded that young man to be the worst version of himself.

But, Thank God, on November 1997 my prayers was answered. Taylor B was born, a little over four pounds with weak lungs, jaundice and purple lips. All that I saw was perfection. As soon as she was born, I left Dub's side and never left Taylor's until the doctors swooped her away from me. I told Dub *"Thank you for my baby."* I looked at my baby girl feeling I had to do everything in my power to give her the world. *No more little boy bullshit games!* This little girl was Godsent. Now this was around the time that shit got real.

I had two baby mamas and had been lying to both of them. Dub had been in the hospital for months trying to stop her preterm labor so it had been easy to keep those two worlds separate. I wanted to keep both and I thought I had no choice, because I didn't want to fall victim to the child support monster that the dudes talked about. Things didn't work out as planned.

They both left my ass high and dry. I can't blame them, I was on some other shit. I can remember when I really started to take being a father for real. The first time I kept Taylor one day all by myself. She was maybe three weeks old and so tiny. I was scared as hell. I'd babysat before but this was MY kid. My daughter. Nobody else's. Watching Taylor looking back at me with wonder I knew I had to get my shit together.

I can't really tell you how Dub and I got back together. But back then we were never really apart. I tried to juggle being father of two at a young age but I failed miserably. I never felt that way with the first kid. I felt like I was babysitting him every time. I can't tell you what it was but I never felt a connection or a deep bond. The crazy part about the whole thing is Dub loved the hell out that little boy. Truth be told she use to make me pick him up and take him for weekends. This shit went on for three years, damn near four.

Things were looking great, money was coming in and life was peach. I was getting the hang of this daddy thang . Taylor was my world. I would come home every night to feed and bathe her. I was doing what some said couldn't be done. I was in the streets and a family man. I spent time with Dub and Taylor and hit licks in between time.

I thought I had it all right, until that night I totally fucked up. #1007450. I'm going to leave that right there for a second. Life changed in a lot of ways after that night. I really felt that night laid the foundation for the rest of Dub and I relationship. I was never the same after that night, my whole way of being changed. I couldn't be me anymore, I was lost. Not only I'm going through that shit this but my baby mama had the nerve to start flexing with me over the little boy. I wanted to say, "Man fuck you." Instead, I took my happy ass down to the child support office and tried to file on myself. Nah I was not high, I was sober as fuck. That is when shit went sideways. I had to take a DNA test to get my rights and shit. During this time #1007450 was getting closer. To add insult to injury, Dub was pregnant again.

I just know for a fact God hated me! It took the DNA forever to come back but oh when it did. The results were 0.0000% chance that I was the father and I lost my mind. I did something that day that some thought was mean and wrong of me. But to tell you the truth that shit felt so fucking good. I was free. One less problem to deal with. One less kid. Shit might change.

Hell, no. I was not that lucky. Now Dub pregnant in the hospital with our second child and I am at home full-time with Taylor alone. #1007450 getting closer by the day. Dub's Aunt Gloria, God bless her soul, because she kept my baby every night. She knew I was a dope boy back then. That was the best place for my baby to be. Oh, and if you're wondering where Dub was, she was my trap queen, cooking up my crack and counting the money. That's another story for another book and time.

In June 2000, my namesake OB4 was born. Once again I didn't have any plans but it was too late by then. I was in my son's life for all of three months before #1007450 caught up to me and held on super tight. I found myself an inmate, #1007450, for over a year. Dub was alone with a toddler and a sick newborn son. I felt helpless in that cell because there was nothing I could do to help her. It was during this time that I made a promise to her that when I was a free man again, we would be married. My boy looked just like me. I felt an immediate bond with him as soon as he was born. I was sick as fuck that I was in a cage and he was out there somewhere without me. Every day I would wake up and tell myself, "I will never be in here again. I got to get my shit together."

The Twins

Now this is when shit really got crazy. We were married for a few years at this time and we were going through some things. Mostly financial, because I didn't have a job. They say most marriages fail the first two to three years due to finances. We were going through a separation (shout out to BJeezy, Dub's best friend, for being so real and subletting your apartment and giving me my first real taste of freedom). One day Dub hit me with *"I want another baby."* I told her *"Oh hell nah! Fuck no. No no no."* Mind you I didn't want to have kids, so the kids we had were two too many for me already. I told her, *"You go do what you want to go do. If another baby will make you happy go do you but it ain't coming from this dick. Nope."* In my mind, we were not getting back together ever again anyway so it didn't matter.

Months pass and we are still fucking around but separated, not really but really, but it slowed down. We didn't see each other for a while so I started messing with this chick, dipping in and out. I was working out of town so I would see her when I came into town and that was that. One day she called me and told me she was pregnant. OH HELL NAH! I told her, *"This ain't the lick, do not have a kid with me. Me and you are two different people."* To this day I thank her for not listening to me because she gave me a gift of a son. He turned out to be my truest version of me and has tested my limits as a parent from day one. Here I am shook to my core because I am married and I got a whole chick over there pregnant for me. I had been through the whole mama's-baby, daddy's-maybe thing before, so my thought was she not my gal. And it is a possibility that I could dodge another bullet like I did before.

Our youngest child, Bill, had an emergency surgery to remove his appendix and Dub called me up to the hospital. While we are talking and getting reacquainted she confessed to me that she was pregnant. *"What the fuck you mean you pregnant? You my muthafuckin' wife fuck you mean you pregnant?"* I asked her as if I didn't have the same news to share. Now, when she told me who she was pregnant for I wanted to snap her muthafucking neck because I didn't like that *n!%%@*. I was tripping but knew both of our feelings were about to be hurt because I had to tell her I had a chick pregnant too. Keep in mind we are still legally married. Dub took the news in stride again. She had my back again and I looked at her in awe because this girl was just not like others.

My grandmother was the closest woman in the world to me and she was sick. Dub was the only person I ever leaned on so as I was accepting my grandmother's last days me and Dub became close again. My grandmother died and I tried to stay home with my grandfather while he was grieving, but the house was just not the same without my favorite girl. I was emotional and told Dub, *"Girl, let's just get back together and make this thing work."* My side piece is pregnant and my wife, who was somebody else's (#2's) side piece was pregnant and we were back together living life. My friends asked. *"How you laid up next her and she pregnant with another man's baby?"* Everybody thought we were crazy. That just goes to show you how crazy-strong our bond was. It wasn't even a lover's bond, it was more a *that's my people bond*. And when my people need me I have to be there for them, for her.

The father of Dub's kid flaked on her early in the pregnancy so we didn't have to deal with him. Dub knew how I was about having more kids and she understood, as always, that we would not leave my other girl's new baby behind and that she would support me. Those two little kids, one boy and one girl, Nicco and Carmela, born less than three months apart, we call them *The Twins*, were conceived in a time of turmoil and from the most fucked up circumstances. But those two babies showed both of us what it truly meant to love someone unconditionally. I can honestly say Carmela, or Peanut as I call her, is my true testimony of love. I love that little girl like that is my flesh and blood. You cannot tell me otherwise, she is my baby. Dub is the same way with Nicco. She acts like she laid upside down in the hospital for two months like she did the others and pushed him out of her own body. You cannot convince her otherwise.

When we say that we *blended families*, we really began in 2005 when *The Twins* were born. Nicco in January and Carmela in April. Outside kids that would have been shunned in any other situation. We broke the mold and did it differently. People tried to convince me that we were living a real life soap opera but that is not how we saw it. We were just living our life. I fucked up, she fucked up. Who fucked up the most? Nobody. We called it even and kept it pushing. To this day, they are still *The Twins*, frick and frack, Thing 1 and Thing 2. They speak their own language and protect one another like they shared a womb together. They get on our nerves sometimes because they are so fucking close. You can't see one without the other. That's *The Twins*, two for one.

It takes a very mature person to deal with that situation. Dub and I grew up a lot during that time. I never thought I would be a man who raised another man's kid. Remember I didn't want kids! Never. It turned out to be the easiest situation and transition that Dub and I went through in our whole marriage. We did not make one another feel guilty, we didn't turn our backs on each other. We were a team. We figured it out and we never used terms like *"step kid."* That is my daughter. That is her son. If you are married to a person, and they have children, then those children are yours. If they are hungry, you will feed them like you feed your own. If they are sick, you care for them like you would care for your own. If you don't you are a fucked up person for showing a difference between children because you didn't make them. Either way, it matters less what terminology you use and more that you step up and care for the children. (If you want to go around calling yourself somebody's "step dad" be my guest.)

Our marriage was not perfect, it was chopped up and screwed from jump. But look what came of all that turmoil. We went through all of that for a reason. *The Twins* are here and everybody's all right. We can all sit around a table as a family. Peanut is my daughter and Nicco is Dub's son. Just like that.

Chapter Four:
Commitment Kinda - *Then comes marriage*

Dub's Story

On October 5, 2001, we got married in a pawn shop.

I wrote that sentence five minutes ago and I am still laughing.

Seriously, we got married at a pawn shop. I left for a lunch break at work and caught the bus to the pawn shop where the ceremony was going to be held. We got married with the pawn shop clerks as witnesses. I caught a cab back to work to finish the day. I was so sad. All of the years we were together, and I was ashamed to tell people, even our children, that he finally married me. I was using his name as mine for years at this point. Hyphenated maiden-fake married name for over 2 years. I remember not feeling any security or joy. I remember being happy that he had finally married me after he made his jailhouse promise to me but I also remember feeling like he was going to take it back. My feeling was spot on.

On paper OB3 and I were married for 10 years and 4 months. We only lived as husband and wife for three and a half total, non-consecutive years. We would separate a year or so, then reconcile. Our longest separation was two years, during which he gave me the freedom to move out of our home and go grow up in the world and pursue the love interest that I was so fixated on, #2, even though he knew that it was not going to end well. It was a disaster in some ways but it was also the most generous thing he had ever done for me. Do you know how much someone has to love you to let you go and pursue a relationship with someone else? He did that for me and I was and still am eternally grateful for that.

I was able to travel and get my emotions under control. I was able to find some direction in my life with goals and meditating. I became closer to God. I got to actually grieve the loss of my mother and release my fear of dying and leaving my children behind. I released so much in that time away from him. All that freedom, but I missed being under the same roof with my children. I talked to my Grandpa Lou, OB3's grandfather, with whom I was extremely close, and he asked me to go back home. He was sick and didn't know what was going to happen and he wanted his family to be strong and intact while he was still around to see. I asked OB3 if I could come home one day out of the blue via text. I fully expected him to cuss me out and laugh in my face. However, that was not the type of man he was. He asked for time and space to think about it and I respected his request. I got the *"Come back home"* text, and I began to shut down my single life and prepare to head back home. I was dating this terrific and amazing man, whom I knew would be hurt by my decision. It was unfair to him, but I wanted to do what Grandpa Lou told me was right. I wanted to try one more time to get this marriage on track.

The first few months were bliss. The kids were adapting, we were enjoying each other's company and we were finally making our house a home. The last time we separated we had just purchased our home in September 2007. I left that December. I'd invested time getting used to this new space, which was uncomfortable to me. I'd worked myself into learning the neighbors, the area, the stores, the schools, everything. But a year into reconciliation, I felt lost again. I had a list of goals and when I was single, I would knock my list down line-by-line. Trying to complete a set of goals for myself with a husband and four children was much harder. I wanted to go back to school, so I enrolled full-time without asking or discussing it with my husband. I spent money on the credit cards and bank accounts like it was mine alone, because for the most part it was. I was the breadwinner. I never included him in any of my decisions. My money, my decisions was my mindset. Horrible, terrible, no good way to be in a marriage. I didn't look to him as a partner or an equal and he didn't treat me like a woman that he was proud to be with.

He resented the fuck out of me for returning as the same person I had been when I left. Our entire marriage he'd been *Mr. Mom*. He cooked, cleaned and cared for our children. He did it very well but I told him that I wanted to change and do that now. And I really did try to be a good housewife. It is hard to be a happy housewife after I had been at work all day. I felt stressed out before I even pulled into the driveway, because the commute to and from work was over an hour one-way. I was stressed about bills and lacked affection and real romantic feelings with my husband. I felt like life was draining from my body. So I stopped trying. I am not saying it like it was OK because it was not. It was my reality and it just was not what OB3 had bought in to when we agreed to get back together. He did not complain, he suffered silently. I knew he was as unhappy as I was. I just didn't know what to do to fix it. He had only one rule and I followed that rule as if my life depended on it because I knew truthfully that it did.

"If you fuck that n!%%@ while his child is under my roof I will kill both of you," he said quietly and honestly on my first night back home. I believed him. #2 was still married to his wife at that time and was not worried about me or our daughter so it was easy to keep my promise.

In year two of reconciliation things had changed for me physically. I was sick but I didn't know how sick. I thought stress was the cause but I was so wrong. I was so miserable because I knew the marriage was winding down. I stressed about it every single day because I honestly did not want to fail. OB3 had basically raised me as a woman. When I lost my mom, he was right there to pick me up and dust me off. I leaned on him so heavily and I knew if we broke up again that it would be last time for us. I kept getting sick though and I couldn't shake it. I would be so tired some days that I couldn't pull myself out of the bed. FOR DAYS! I would bleed for weeks. There was a ringing in my ear like a high pitch whistle that was louder than my thoughts. I went to many doctors and got many different diagnoses. I remember going to the OB/GYN for my bleeding and OB3 called me on my way home.

"Hey, how did the appointment go?" He nervously asked.

"It was ok. She ran a bunch of tests." I responded.

"Tests. Did everything come back ok?" He quizzed.

I got quiet. I knew that tone of voice and the reality hit me like a ton of bricks. He was cheating, and he wanted to make sure my illness was not his fault. I hung up the phone without saying a word to him and I just cried. I cried as if my life was completely over because I knew he was gone already. I had failed.

To make matters worse, he wasn't affectionate towards me. *My God*! No kisses. No hugs. We had a handshake to greet one another. Imagine, a handshake with my husband like he was my homeboy! We still use that damn handshake to this day when we greet one another. One thing that I learned from our marriage, especially during this time, was that I was not perfect. Even though I was intelligent, went to work every day and made a great salary, which helped us move out of the hood, I sucked as his wife.

My relationship with our children was nothing like their relationship with their dad. I was so disconnected and focused on work and achieving goals while he was on the floor sword fighting with our daughter or teaching our son how to get to the next level on a video game. His affection towards them was open and always available. I used to watch them and feel jealous. Seriously, a true pang of jealousy would hit because I wish I had a dad that loved me like OB3 loved his children. Truth be told, I wished OB3 loved me as he loved his children. The only time we touched was to have sex and that was so infrequent that I was starving for the physical touch of a man.

Another thing that I learned during this time was that a marriage can be irreparably broken. My ego could not accept that hard truth at first, but it was true. I knew when he married me that he was not doing it because he loved me to death and wanted to grow old with me. I could not even picture OB3 and I old together! I married him because he was my best friend. He was like my big brother in many ways, a big brother that I happened to have sex with every once in a while. I know that sounds so twisted now saying it aloud, but it was how I felt.

I suffered so horribly from anxiety that panic attacks became a regular part of my life. So when I began to faint, bleed heavily, lose weight, and rarely get out of bed I just assumed it was a by-product of my anxiety. I was very wrong. I was actually dying and didn't know it. On December 26th, I was sick of being in his presence because he stayed out most of the night on Christmas with his 'friends'. The disrespect was mounting and I was tired of it. To avoid having to be around him, I decided to get up and run errands the next day even though I could barely stand. I passed out running those errands and life changed for me forever after that day. An ambulance rushed me to the nearest hospital and I was surrounded by doctors and nurses trying to keep me alive. It took the doctors almost a week to finally diagnose me with a rare bone marrow disease called Aplastic Anemia. This disease presents itself the same as blood cancer without the cancer cells. Doctors told me I was not leaving the hospital anytime soon, I had to undergo chemo and recover. Everything moved so fast after that and our breakup got pushed to the back burner as I focused on surviving.

OB3 was not there by my side every day, mostly because he couldn't be. He would call to check on me or bring me clothes, but for the most part he just took care of the children and went to work. I knew he was scared but so was I. There was not much I could do to help him. After a few months in the hospital, it was time for me to go home. Anxiety crept back in because I knew

OB3 wanted out but I knew I needed him now more than ever. I asked him on my last night in the hospital if I should go stay with Grandpa Lou and give him some space. He told me, *"No. Come home. I will get you well. We will talk about us later."* He kept his word.

In hindsight, OB3 and I had no idea what we were doing. We were kids when we got married. We didn't have any examples of marriage to glean from except Grandpa Lou and Grandma Millie, but they were old, and we didn't pay attention. My idea of marriage came from the Cosby Show. His idea of marriage came from the streets. That just lets you know how far removed we were from one another. But, he was all I knew.

My mom was dead and he was the only man who had known that part of me and my life. The man who had raised me as his own, Uncle Ernie, was dead. My aunt Meme who had spoiled me to death was dead. My uncle James and I were not on speaking terms. My baby sister was living her young life. I didn't want to lose OB3. He was the only family I had left. Neither of us was prepared for marriage, nor did we take it seriously. It wasn't our style to talk things out. That would have been mature. Instead, one of us would get pissed off at some small and insignificant thing the other did, we'd separate until we missed each other and then we were back together. That was our pattern and it was the worst thing I think we did to our babies. We let them see the dysfunction of breaking up and making up for YEARS. The last time we did this they were old enough to look at us like the fools we were as we moved my things back into our house.

Marriage is the real deal. OB3 and I failed horribly at it. Egos, inexperience and lack of communication killed our marriage before it had started. Our children were the only great things to come of our union, and the funny thing is both of our biological children were born *before* we got married. The children that were born after marriage were conceived with different people. Oh yes, we did the damn fool. I do not regret my marriage with OB3 because he taught me about myself and when it ended I vowed to never just exist in a marriage or relationship ever again. My ex-husband taught me that even though I had done so much work on myself, I still had some more work to do. I needed to learn to love myself as much as, if not more, than I loved a man. That is how the universe works, you repeat the same lessons until you learn the true meaning of each.

OB3's Story

Man! Let me just tell y'all, being married is way trickier than people make it out to be. It is not THAT hard but there is a sweet science to it. When I got married to Dub I was dumb as fuck, had no business doing it, and didn't know what I was doing. I really did not want to get married but I felt obligated to get married. Marrying out of obligation instead of pure love is the worst thing you can do. Now did I love her? Yeah. But was I 'in love' with her to justify getting married. Hell nah. I loved the streets more than her back then. I was being young and dumb. She just happened to be there holding me down when I was locked up and feeling like shit. She put up with my bullshit all those years. All the jump-offs, going back and forth and 'baby mama drama. The least I could do was give her my last name. Wrong decision.

The day we got married, we went home and she went to the bedroom to read a book and I sat on the couch, rolled up a joint and watched ESPN. What a hell of a honeymoon! We should have known things were going to be fucked from there. We were unbalanced from the beginning. On one end, you have a wife who goes to work every day to make ends meet. Then on the other end, you have a husband trying to do different hustles, pretending to be something more than he was, in the streets, at that time. It didn't matter how she saw me but it did matter how the streets saw me. I was faking and shaking and not making much bread. So, she had a reason to be pissed all the time. She was making the bread, I was not. My solution to the money gap was to become *Mr. Dad.* I pretended I couldn't find a job when really I was not looking. I felt like shit, but figured if she went to work and came home without needing to cook, clean or handle the children then I was doing my part. Unfortunately, in this society, at that time, it was not respectable for a man to play the househusband role. In my opinion, I played a major part, but it was not the proper balance for us. The rules and the picking order were never really established in the proper way. I wanted to be the respected boss, but I couldn't pay a bill. To my fellas, if you can't pay the bills then you can't be the boss. You really don't have any business putting your dick in any woman if you're broke. Instead you should be focused on generating an income.

I got sidetracked.

Dub and I tried to make it work. I felt her love for me but it was more like a platonic love. We'd known one another for so long, I figured we give it a shot. And we played the game as long as we could before we realized it wasn't a game at all. A few years in to the marriage we separated for the first time. During that separation, we began having children with other people.

In order to be married you have to be willing to sacrifice a bunch of shit and let go of past attachments and situations. You have to be willing to put the needs of your family before your own. You even have to be willing to share whatever you have. I'm not just speaking about property or money, I am talking about sharing yourself, your emotions, your ups and downs, good times and bad. I know this is going to be tough for some of the men to hear and accept, but you should be able to cry and be vulnerable with your significant other and family. Understand, if you are with someone who will use your weakness against you that is not the one you're meant to be with. If you're hopping into a marriage solely because you have been dating this person for fifteen years or because you have four kids together, the marriage is almost certain to fail, fam. You have to be sure you're getting married for the right reasons or your foundation will be weak.

To me, love is a very strange thing, it can't be explained. Being married means you have to really love your partner to the extent that being away from them makes you feel incomplete. You need to love them so strongly you need their presence, their touch, their smell. You must be willing to tell them everything about you. I am remarried now and I have told my wife about all of my THOT-ing ass ways back in the day, how I used to be a pure male whore. It felt good to be able to share those details about my past comfortably. That is my wife, that is my best friend. I have friends that I have known so long that we used to play marbles together, and I can tell her more than I can tell them. I am more vulnerable with her and I would rather share my innermost feelings with her than anybody. If you have a friend or someone outside the marriage whom you can talk to more than your spouse, then you are in the wrong marriage.

You have to be mentally and emotionally ready to take on your spouse's issues, problems, dark moments as well as all their good. You can't pick and choose. If she is ten million dollars in debt, now you are ten million dollars in debt too. If he has four kids by four baby mamas, now you have four kids and four baby mamas, too. If you are not ready for that then kick rocks, do not put a ring on that finger. A piece of paper, a ring and a recited speech is not going to make you a husband or a wife. You don't become a husband or wife because of a ceremony or a ring. It has to come from a deeper place of love and commitment inside of you. At the time that we were married, Dub and I, weren't husband-and-wife material, because neither of us was willing to commit to the highest possible level.

Don't step into the realm of marriage until you are truly ready. It affects more than just you, especially if you have children. Sweet baby Jesus, if there are kids involved, please make sure you are ready to do the right things. And, don't marry just because your grandma, mama or daddy likes the person. They won't have to live with that person every day. If you don't love them AND like them on that level, hold off on marriage, real talk patna. Marry who is best for you. I don't give two flying fucks if the world doesn't like them, if you love them that is all that matters. Be happy with who you are with. And, if you aren't happy, don't wait. End it now. Do NOT get married or stick around for the children. Your babies are going to grow up and move on with their lives. Then you're going to look like an ass in a forty-year marriage with a person you don't even like. That's like serving a forty-year prison sentence.

Depression and resentment will set in earlier than you can imagine. Marriage and your mental health are nothing to play with or take lightly. It seems everyone wants the title or to flash to the ring. But those don't mean a goddamn thing if you have to go home to someone you don't like every night. I hear people say, *"Sometimes I like her, sometimes I don't."* I said, *"Either you like her or you don't."* I've found that like will carry you a lot further than love. My grandpa Lou used to tell Dub and me during his many lectures, *"I don't want somebody who just loves me I want somebody who cares about me and likes me too. You might stop loving me, but if you care about me and like me you will always make sure I am ok."*

I played around with my first marriage, thinking I was doing something cute. I thought it was going to make me look legit to the boys in the hood. Settling down and getting married would make me look more stable and honest in the whole world's eyes. Even though I had no intention of doing right by Dub from day one. It looked good. I knew I wasn't going to be a good husband and I was right.

I am glad I got married early because it taught me a lot about myself. It showed me my many shortcomings. It exposed me as an imperfect man. I walked around with an attitude like any woman would be lucky to have me. At times, I had great intentions, but without actions intentions mean nothing. My marriage with Dub taught me how I was letting past issues hinder my development as a man. My bad habits were preventing me from loving or caring for anybody. I didn't see it then, but I see it now in my current marriage. I am constantly growing, I am not perfect, but I did learn that. In our ten-year marriage I got a doctorate degree in relationship education.

I experienced first-hand how I could go from really liking a woman to really despising her and her presence. Dub and I are cool as a fan now, but there was a time that I did not want to see her face walk through the door. It ruined my whole vibe. That wasn't marriage. That's not life for anybody. If you are going through that with your spouse it is time to have a come to Jesus moment and lay it all out on the table. Say, *"I really don't like you. I prefer to be anywhere but home. What we going to do? What needs to change?"*

If you have to change who you are fundamentally to be in the marriage then it's time to move on. If you look in the mirror and don't recognize the man or woman that you have become, then it is time to ask yourself some tough questions. *Why did you let it get that far gone? Why didn't you share your feelings with the person with whom you shared vows?*

There is more to marriage than the wedding day. There will be days that are heaven and then there will be days that make Hurricane Harvey look like a spring shower. You are going to have to go through some things. The ups and the downs. Don't allow yourself to get lost in the beauty of your marriage, because when the ugly aspects of married life come up you won't be able to handle the shock of it. Expect to take the good with the bad. When you are up, enjoy it but don't make too much of it. When you are down, get through it by getting your ass back up. Marriage is a partnership. And it is not 50/50. It's 100/100. It is you and your spouse LITERALLY against the world.

If your spouse is your true partner, he or she will be willing to go up against God for you. No blasphemy intended, but that is how tight that partnership has to be in order to rock with this marriage thing. I was not ready for that level of commitment and intimacy when I married Dub. I took on a responsibility I wasn't ready for. Marriage is a bigger responsibility than becoming a parent. When you become a parent, you have more control, you can mold that child. On the other hand, taking on the responsibility of another adult, with his or her own mind, own way of being, own thoughts can be dangerous. You are taking on a responsibility of something you do not have control over. Are you willing to take that risk and give up that control?

Women, y'all say the man is supposed to lead, but if he's lost he cannot logically lead you. Fellas, if you're leading, understand your woman isn't your blind follower, she's your navigator. *Baby I want to go here, can you read this map and tell me how to get us there?* Do you trust she can she read the map to get you where you want to go? Or is she only good for looking cute, turning you on and agreeing to everything you say and do. You can't go far with a woman like that. If she is reading the map and says, *"Baby I found a better route,"* are you certain her discernment will get you where you're going? You have to be able to feed off of each other. If you can't, one is going to feed off the other like a vampire until there is nothing left. One of you will be fat and the other will be devoured. If your partner is not adding to you they are subtracting from you.

Take marriage seriously, don't do it out of pride or obligation. Pure love, pure desire and being IN love is what it takes to make a marriage work. If you cannot look at your partner without wanting to change them then you may end up wasting years of your life marrying them. You can get anything back except for your time. We wasted ten years of our lives.

Chapter Five:
D-I-V-O-R-C-E - *Unhappily ever after*

Dub's Story

OB3 and I were married for ten years on paper. We lived together for a total of three and a half of those 10 years as husband and wife. Although we would break up and make up all the time, I knew for a fact that the last breakup was our final ride. Why? He initiated the divorce. He was not angry or sad. He was matter-of-fact and there was no changing his mind.

The reconciliation had happened 18 months prior to the final breakup. Living apart all those years changed both of us without our realizing it. During the last breakup, I moved out and left our two children full-time with him while I took time to regroup, recoup and rediscover life. Prior to the divorce, I had been diagnosed with an autoimmune disease called Aplastic Anemia. The diagnosis came as we were growing apart. In retrospect, I feel that my disease had a huge part to play in the final breakup. I was too tired to be a wife, a mom, a friend. I had never been too good at that when I was healthy. I knew he was growing tired of me being so disconnected and checked out from life. Plus, I was making reckless decisions with money and other things, so he was tired of me all around. I could not prove it, I never did prove it, but I strongly suspected him of cheating on me again. He was rarely home. He went out with 'friends' so much it was like he'd moved out this time. On the day I passed out and was rushed to the hospital, we were so disconnected my first call in the hospital was not to my husband. I called my grandpa instead.

After my long stay in the hospital OB3 got me home. He got me stronger. He took care of me when I needed to be taken care of and he pushed me to take care of myself when I could. He was not cruel towards me. He was there and I knew he didn't want to be. I pushed for marriage counseling because after facing death I had put things into perspective that were all out of focus before. My family was all I had, and he was part of that family. He attempted marriage counseling but it didn't work for two reasons. First, counseling and talking to people about feelings wasn't his thing. Second, he was already checked out of the marriage. There was no pulling him back in. We sat on the couch at one of our counseling sessions and I recall being very emotional because things were becoming increasingly strained between us. I do not recall what the therapist said, but I do remember him turning to me and looking at me straight on.

"I want a divorce," he stated without emotion like he was ordering food from a drive-thru.

I stood still because I felt like if I moved the moment would be validated. I began begging. Pleading. Begging, crying and pleading. I ended up on the floor I was so hurt and confused by his declaration. I knew we were on shaky grounds and he barely saw me as a friend at that point, but divorce? After all these years? Why? I did not get it.

"Get up. Have some dignity," the therapist chastised as OB3 began to walk out of the door.

The decision was made. I needed to learn to deal with and accept it. This was the end. I went back to work in a daze. The minutes and hours passed so slowly that I was convinced time had stopped. I called my best friend, Kendra, on the ride home to cry my heart out. I sobbed and yelled and ached on the phone so long that she told me to pull over, she was coming to me. (My tribe is live like that.) Over the next few days, I slowly began to accept my reality. Funny thing is, OB3 was stone. He did not move in any direction. He was not mean. He was not nice. He was neutral. Finally, after days of watching me cry he agreed to have a talk.

"If I have to be the bad guy, so be it. Neither one of us is happy. I am letting you go, so you can go find happiness," he explained to me, stoically. I sobbed, I begged some more and then I went quiet.

Now, here is the crazy thing, neither of us moved out of the house. We lived together under the same roof with the children for some time. He stayed in the master bedroom and I moved upstairs. He would come home from his weeks on the rig at work and spend time with the children. We were cordial, no yelling or name calling. We were essentially roommates. Until one day I saw his laptop and the screen saver was another woman. Oh no! I could accept that it was over, but he could not rub it in my face like that. I put him out. He quietly packed his things while the children were at school and I was at work and left. A neighbor called to report to me that she'd seen him leaving but, the reality of the breakup did not hit me until I walked in the house and the TV and Playstation were gone. *Sidenote: ladies, if he takes the Playstation, he is gone.*

I tried to straighten up the house and closet before the children made it home from school so it did not look so obvious. I needed cleaning supplies so I left to go to the nearest store. Unfortunately, I did not make it back home before the children and our oldest daughter saw that her dad had moved out without an explanation. Honestly, that was the hardest night I have ever had as a parent. The wail that came from my daughter's gut was so piercing and painful, she was so angry and hurt, and there was absolutely nothing I could do to fix that for her. She would not let me hold her even though she would not leave my side. She just cried and her siblings sat around her saying nothing just being present. It was in that moment that my heart turned on OB3. In all of our breakups, I never felt this anger boiling inside of me. I never wished harm on him before that day. I wanted him dead in a casket as I watched our baby girl's heart break. After that night, I made a big mistake. I turned into a victim. Everything became about how he hurt me. I would talk about it to anyone who would listen.

"He left me while I was sick."

"He left me for another woman."

"He left me when he finally got money."

"He left me. He left me. He left me. Woe is me."

My daughter was watching me whither away emotionally and physically. My son was retreating within himself to deal with the breakup. I walked in our house one day and saw the heavy cloud of pain that was hanging over all of us. In that moment, I made the decision to go to family counseling. We needed it desperately. Within a few days we were sitting on the couch with Dr. Keith, a handsome, charismatic black man who was educated and relatable. He immediately made us feel comfortable and we dove into the business of picking up the pieces of our lives.

The mistakes I made early in the breakup weighed heavily on my children. My oldest daughter thought the divorce was her fault because she told her dad it would be ok if he left. My son thought he had to become the man of the house at the tender age of 11. The 18 months they spent living with their dad had left them so attached to him that my presence had become an irritant to them. OB3 and the children were a strong team. They missed him so much when he left they didn't know how to deal with the absence. Once a week we spent two to three hours with our therapist, together and separately. The family met for an hour, then I met with him alone for an hour and afterward the children met with him alone for another hour. It was so intense that some nights we would all leave in tears, silent and unsure if we wanted to return the next week for more.

Meanwhile, OB3 had found a place to live and was picking the children up every weekend he was in town. He would also take the children to school most mornings because he lived close by. I had no idea where he lived. I never asked for an address. I knew he would never put the children in danger, so I didn't need one. During this time, we barely spoke. Text messages were short and business-only. I didn't hate him I was just angry that he ended it after all the shit we had been through. If I never had the courage to pull the trigger how could he? We came up with an acceptable amount of financial support for the children. At least we could agree on the children. They were our main focus. As the children came out of their emotional shells, OB3 and I both exhaled because they seemed to be OK.

During this time, I began to live again. I traveled a lot. Weekend trips to different cities every other weekend while the children were with their dad became my vice. I craved the sound of his wheels pulling up as I took off on another adventure. I would travel alone or with friends. I did not care. I visited many places in an attempt to find myself again since I was no longer defined by my relationship with my children's dad. I would land in a new city and become a totally different person. My name changed with the city. It was fun roaming around, discovering new foods and sights. Then when Sunday came, I'd be back on a plane returning to my real life. I cherished my weekends without the children. I don't care what anybody says, every parent needs some me-time. It took me a almost three decades to learn the importance of self-care. There is nothing in this world like a hotel bed and a map to explore. I was grateful to OB3 for allowing me to have this type of freedom.

Then, one day, he stopped coming to pick up the children regularly. One weekend missed turned into two weekends. Initially, I didn't get too upset. The children seemed OK so we would just re-plan the weekends and do something together. The direct communication with the children did not stop so I figured he needed some time. I gave him that. Weeks turned to months and all of a sudden their dad was gone. Now I was pissed because I was completely in the dark and assumed he was off living a kid-free life. I thought maybe he had moved on and was dating someone. I thought he was finally tired of having child support garnished from his check. Dozens of theories ran through my head but I never picked up the phone to call to ask him what had happened. I just let time pass.

Eventually, our oldest daughter, Taylor, began to resent her dad. My sons missed their dad, but didn't want to tell me because they thought it would upset me. The family dynamics, in the home, had changed drastically. Yet I watched them mourn their dad's absence. I didn't reach out to my friend OB3 during this time because truthfully I did not know what to say. I let him roam without the children. It was over between us and I was no longer in a position to get him back on the right path like I used to do.

Two and a half years passed before he called me one day, out of the blue. By then, I'd re-married and my heart was deeply torn between my husband, whom I loved with my whole soul, and my old friend whom I had shared an entire lifetime with. In this conversation, OB3 did something that I never expected to happen in my life. He apologized to me.

"Dub, I know I was not the best husband to you. I let you down many times. I just couldn't be who you needed me to be. You saw so much in me and I just couldn't be what you saw in me at the time," he started. *"I let you carry the heavy burden of our family alone for a long time. I left everything up to you. I was not a husband to you. I owe you an apology for all of it."*

That day we hugged in the park and talked about his depression, his joblessness, his journey since we'd last seen one another. The man who stood before me that day was not the same man who had divorced me. He was humble, kind, understanding and apologetic. Tears flow freely right now as I type this because that day was a turning point for me and OB3 as parents. Although most people would not understand his absence, I did. When I was tired and had checked out from life, he took the children for me and let me get myself together. Now the tables were turned and I knew I had to forgive him for his absence. I think we both healed the wounds from our divorce that day as we cried, talked and laughed. I had my friend back.

Now, it was time to put the children first and co-parent.

OB3's Story

The divorce was some crazy shit, but it was some shit that I knew, in my gut, had to go down. We had gone too many years going back-and-forth, loving each other, hating each other. We didn't really hate each other but we did hate parts of each other that were never going to change. Fuck it. Sometimes you have to let go. If you love it, you have to let it go. I knew I had hit the point where I couldn't keep playing Boo Boo The Fool.

I knew where she wanted to be and no matter what I did or how much I changed it was not going to change the status of me in her heart. I was number two in her heart and I eventually accepted that. Sometimes as a man you have to put pride aside and accept that, *"Shit my n!%%@, your best wasn't good enough. You did what you had to do and it was not good enough."*

I think the nail in the coffin was when we tried to do that marriage counseling bullshit, which I was totally against. I knew it was a total waste of time. But I did the dumb shit. Went to a couple sessions, watched some stupid ass movie I didn't give a flying fuck about all in the name of saving a marriage that was already doomed in my mind. I went through the steps. In counseling, the therapist asked Dub, *"What is the one thing you resent most about OB3 hanging out so much with his friends."* Dub looked me in my face and said *"You are not loyal."* In my 41 years of life I have been called a lot of names.

Dirty muthafucka.

Sorry muthafucka.

No good muthafucka.

Rotten muthafucka.

Out of all the crazy shit I had ever done, no one told me I was a disloyal person. So for her to say, after all those years, of me putting up with a bunch of shit that I really didn't have to, doing a bunch of shit when I didn't have to, standing up for her when I didn't have to. For her to say I was disloyal to her, that was it for me. I could look past a lot of shit. For her, I was willing to look past a lot of shit. But being labeled disloyal after all the shit I went through with her, nah I couldn't look past that.

That was the divorce.

There was no bitter shit. I was not mad. That is the crazy part about it. I was just like ok it is what it is. All I wanted from it was a peace of mind, my Playstation, my TV and my car. I felt like with those couple of things I would be alright. *"Shit. We gone play this however it is gone play, get this paperwork signed and I am back free on these streets."* The divorce went well. I can't say I lost anything financially. Yeah I lost my family but most boys were getting raped and dragged over coals in divorce. Divorce will have *n!%%@s* looking bad and struggling out there in those streets. But for us it never got to that point. We agreed on everything and it all went as planned.

I knew in the back of my mind which way she was going to go afterward. I was uncomfortable with the choice I knew she would make and was sure it would fail. I honestly wasn't hating on that *n!%%@*. Nah. It wasn't any of that, *"Ah man you got my wife."* It was the individual. I knew him and his pure ho tendencies. But, sometimes you have to give people what they are asking for just to let them see it ain't worth it. For real you gotta let em go. You gotta let a muthafucka bump their head. She was just like my child. If my child tried to touch that stove I can tell after endless warnings, one day I'd have to say fuck it and let them burn their hand. They know now why you said don't touch it. She knows now why I said he is a pure bitch. I still hate that she got burned the way she did, but it had to happen. She had to touch that muthafucking stove.

I am not saying I was innocent in all of this. I could have done better as a husband. I was never taught, I never saw a blueprint and neither did she. I did see how to be a piss poor parent. So I knew what not to do. But did I fall short? Hell yeah, I fell short plenty of times. I ain't no perfect muthafucka and I ain't gonna claim to be one. When it comes to the parenting, this shit here is an art. You gotta do what you gotta do and you gotta roll how you gotta roll.

When it comes to being with someone for damn near 20 years and then going your separate ways you really can't be out here flexing and showing too much emotion towards the situation. Yeah you may be mad, but if you know you're going to overreact, then you have to remove yourself from the situation. It might sound fucked up, but it's what I did. I had to pull back and let the situation between Dub and #2 play out. I knew some people might look at me sideways for doing it the way I did. Sometimes you have to look bad to look good in the end and so nobody can say you interfered or that their fuck up was your fault.

Parenting is a delicate balance. I am not saying that it was the right thing to do. It was a hell of a sacrifice I had to make. My absence was not purely because of her situation with #2. I had lost my family and a really good job in the span of less than two years. I went through a bout of depression. I was just feeling low. I had lost too much. Too quick. Any *n!%%@* can take a loss but those were big hits. A *n!%%@* had to really bounce back from those L's. It was not the easiest thing to do. During that time I am sure there was some crazy shit said about me. OB3 this. OB3 that. At the end of the day I didn't give a fuck. I never really did put a lot of weight on other people's opinions of me. Like you reading this right now, you are forming an opinion of me right now. That's cool. Good? Bad? I really don't give a fuck either way because who are you to judge me or my actions?

Divorce and children. You must understand a divorce is a grown up decision. Divorce is two adults deciding not to be together anymore. Ok, cool beans. But don't be petty and involve your children in it. All of a sudden, the ex is a piss poor parent and can't be around the children? Or when we together we spent $500 a month on the child now you need $2000 in child support for the same child because we're no longer together? Get off the gas! Stop using these children as tools and weapons in your petty war.

By the same token, while you are getting out of dodge, don't leave your children behind. It doesn't matter that you aren't married anymore. That's still your child! If you leave your child behind and NEVER try to go back then you are a pure bitch. Your ex will eventually move on and start entertaining other people. You need to sit down and have a conversation with him or her about what you think is and is not acceptable regarding your child. Talk about it with you ex like an adult. But you can't say *"My children can't come around you because you have these hos around them."* That is no longer your place. If those hos are not busting your children upside the head or doing anything inappropriate around your child, then it is none of your business who is at your ex's house. Stop involving your children in your petty emotional drama. They are already taking an L. They are used to seeing their parents every day, together, in what they called home. Now they don't have that anymore. Every day is an L for them. Don't make it worse for them.

Some of you dirty muthafuckas go out of your way to to take a dig at the other parent, not understanding that it is harming your child. It is fucking with them. Don't be spiteful with your child, trying to get back at the ex because your feelings are hurt. Your feelings being hurt momentarily will have a lifelong effect on the children. Yes, it hurts today but eventually you will move on. Next thing you know you will be on cloud 9 and all that hurt fades. But the child still does not have his mama and daddy everyday like before. Do you ever take that into consideration? Or are you too busy trying to get revenge? *"He got a new bitch, I am going to go get me a new n!%%@."* Or, *"She got a new n!%%@, I am going to get me a new bitch."* That shit ain't cool.

We always telling children to stay in a child's place yet you want to drag them into grown folk business by forcing them to watch the drama and pick sides? You put a child in adult shit and now they have to behave as an adult. You cannot pick and choose when you want the child to be a child. You want to tell them adult shit and put them in adult business and then when your child has an opinion you want to tell them, *"Stay in a child's place."* Nah. You should have kept them out of your pettiness from jump.

Just because a breakup happened does not mean that the other parent is no longer fit to be around the child. They were fit to make the child with, remember? So, fuck that. If they were cool enough to be around the children when you were together, then they are cool enough to be around the children now. If they are not fit to be around the children, prove that. Fellas, you can go to court too. Don't listen to the lies that the mama always wins. It is not true, that is just an excuse. If you can't prove your case to a judge, then be ready to eat shit and share the children with their mom.

Bottom line: be happy for other people happiness. It will bring you happiness.

Chapter Six:
From the mouth of babes

Carmela - 13 years old

My mom went through the divorce with my bonus dad, OB3, and it took a huge toll on mom and my bonus dad for a long time. I was only four years old so I don't remember very much about the divorce except mom was sad, Taylor was mad, Nicco was needy, Bill was confused and we didn't see my bonus dad very much for a long time. I do remember going to see a man named Dr. Clarke because he had a cool house with a pool in the backyard. He was nice and he would tell us ways to talk to our mom about our feelings. As we got older my mom and bonus dad started working on blending our family with my dad and my sisters. It was not that easy because my real dad didn't like that I still loved my bonus dad and wanted to see him and hang out with him. That made me very sad but my mom told me to follow my heart and that I should not worry about the grown people's mess.

OB3 and my mom became good friends again and that is when we started to see him more and talk to him more again. I love talking to him and listening to his accent. He makes me laugh and he lets me know how much he really loves me all the time. I feel like my own dad treats me different than my other sisters but OB3 never treats me any different than any of the kids. To him, I'm just Peanut.

My bonus dad got married recently to a really cool woman named My and she has two kids, so I have another big brother and little sister. We get to go to their house and spend time with them often. It is LIT how our families are able to come together and have a phenomenal time. We all chill, laugh, play and nobody has to worry about hurting anyone's feelings. Now that I am old enough to really understand I think my mom and bonus dad blending our families was the best choice after getting a divorce. It made us really happy to see our parents happy as friends. I hope one day I can see the same thing with my mom, dad and sisters.

-CC the Kid

Nicco - 13 yrs old

I don't remember the marriage or the divorce. I was only four years old. One day I lived with my real mom, my big sister and brother. Then I lived with my dad, my new mom, my brother and sisters. Then, one day, it was just my new mom, my brother and sisters. They tell me stories about how I used to sit at the bottom of the stairs and just cry until Taylor would come and take care of me. CC (Carmela) was the only person that I could talk to. I was scared to talk to mama because she was so sad all the time. Then we started going to family counseling and I hated it because I did not want to talk. I just wanted to play and watch tv.

One day mama was OK. We started going places and doing stuff again as a family without my dad. I didn't know him that well so I didn't really have much to miss. I always wondered when he was coming back because I wanted to know him. When he started picking us up again I was so happy, but then he stopped. That is when I got real mad. CC and I went to the same school and I would get in trouble every single day. Sometimes the teacher would tell CC and she would not tell mama. Sometimes they would call mama at work and she would have to leave to come get me. I was just mad and didn't care what I was doing.

Mama asked me why I did the things I did? I always gave the same answer, *"I don't know."* My dad came back in our life when I was in fifth grade. He introduced all of us to his new girlfriend and her kids. They were cool. My dad was cool too. He had lots of stories to tell. I liked to go over to their house on the weekends, but I hated coming home. My mama's new husband always made me feel bad about being happy to see my real dad. He would be my friend all week long but then when I came back from my dad's house he was not cool anymore. I hated that. Mama asked me if I wanted to go live with my dad. I did not want to leave my school, friends and siblings so I told her no but I was sick of her husband acting like knowing my dad was a bad thing. I was frustrated. She promised me she would take care it. A few months later he was gone.

Now, it is good having a blended family because we get to spend a lot of time together. Our family is real cool because we all get along very well. I have two new siblings and my dad's wife is the best. I have three parents now and they all have different personalities. I can go to each of them and get different advice on school, basketball, anything really. I play basketball and I felt like a champion seeing and hearing my entire family in the bleachers cheering me on when my team was playing. It made me play even harder! I am glad that I have mama to take such good care of me every day and my dad whenever I need him. If I had to choose I would pick having a blended family over not seeing my dad at all.

-Pops

Billy- 17 yrs old

I don't remember much from my parents' divorce, I was in the fifth grade when it happened. I only remember the constant fighting and arguing over things I knew nothing about. I remember in the beginning of 5th grade I had a science lab where we were learning about lab safety and we had to do a project over it. I probably was the worst child when it came to school out of Taylor, CC, and myself. At the beginning of that year I was making my way doing good in class, staying out of trouble and actually doing my work. One night I was in the living room working on my lab safety project and while I was working on it I could hear my parents fighting. I remember this fight as the worst I had ever heard them.

After about an hour into doing my project and listening to my parents yell at each other as loud as possible I finished and wanted to show them. I knocked on the door happy and eager to show them what I'd done, but they couldn't hear my child-size knocks over their yelling. I sat at their door for nearly an hour waiting for the fighting to stop so I could show them my poster board. When I finally got to show them the poster it was about 9:30 at night and I had forgotten what I was waiting for. When they came out of the room, my mother's face was as red as an apple even though she is brown, and I could tell she'd been crying. As she looked at what I done she could barely smile at it. My dad didn't even get a chance to look because he was in the closet doing what I could tell was packing up his things and getting ready to leave.

Less than a month after that fight my father moved into a new home. I came home from school one day and things different. He would normally be in his room or in the living room watching football. I went into my parent's room looking for him.

But that day, his red laptop which would usually be on the bed, along with his TV, PS3 and clothes were all gone. I called him scared, thinking we had been robbed for a second time, only for him to tell me *"Nah son, I left but good looking out."*

I was only 10 and didn't know what the hell to do or say so I told him ok and hung up the phone. I did not know that was the last time I would speak to him for almost 3 months. Taylor knew way more than I did about what was actually happening, because while I was calm and ok with what was going on, Taylor and mom were breaking down in different ways. Mom was downstairs throwing glass cups at the wall, burning pictures and fighting walls while Taylor was laying in her bed crying her soul out like someone had just passed away. Nothing about my father moving out and my parents getting a divorce actually got to me until I met Dr. Keith. I was labeled as a 'troubled child' not understanding, until I was older, how my father leaving played a part in how I behaved since the 5th grade. Dr. Clarke helped me realize what was going on around me and see why I was acting the way I was. With his help I was able to let go of the anger and miserable feeling I had inside of me.

Over the next three or four years of my life seeing my father was like finding a "Legendary Scar" on Fortnite. It rarely happened. I would only see him in person once or twice a year. I'd hear from him on social media on my birthdays and Christmas only and very little in any other form of communication. Although I would barely see or hear from him, I never lost my love for him or the hope that he would be back in our life like he never left. I could never hold his leaving against him because I was left out of almost everything related to the split including the reasons behind it, so I didn't know who did what or who had asked for the split. I blamed my dad not being in my life on my mother with the belief that she hated him and didn't want him anywhere near me or my sister. The way my mother would speak of him during this time period only further reinforced my idea, because when I would bring him up or talk about him she would be quick to dismiss the conversation and tell me that my dad was the reason I couldn't see him. Every time she would say that I would get angry and swear that she was lying and just didn't want me to be with him. When she introduced her new man, I never got too close. I wanted my father and that was what it was.

This habit my step dad had of talking bad on the man that gave me his name made me never believe anything he or she would say about my dad. Even at times I wanted to move out and go live with him because I believed life would be much better. That all went away in the second semester of my freshmen year of high school. I knew it was changing when me, Taylor, CC, Nicco and my mom had a conversation about how her and my father finally came to an agreement about us going and seeing him at his new home in Humble. First we had to meet his girlfriend,

My. We met her in the Fall of 2016 at a park in Cypress. We had no clue what to expect when we came to this meeting. The only thing we know about her was she was my dad's 'lady friend' and had kids. We didn't even know what she looked like, her race, height, anything. We were sitting at the park looking for her, pointing at every red car that drove by saying it was her. At one point CC thought she was a fat Asian lady.

When we finally met the right person we didn't realize we were meeting our future bonus mom and an important part of the way our lives would change over the next few years. After meeting My I got to meet her oldest child Demetrius. I never thought I would meet someone so much like me in just about every way except his nasty taste in football teams, but he probably got that from his mother whose taste is even worse. We finally met My's baby Maddie who was scared to talk to me and Nicco until about the third time we hung out.

Within a month of our first meeting we were already staying the night at my dad's house every weekend, spending any free time we had getting to know the newest members of our family. Being able to call and see my father every weekend like I do now, being able to talk to him whenever I'm bored or talk to about things that boys are supposed to tell their fathers is a feeling I never realized how much I missed until I got it back. I was still torn because I felt it was uncomfortable for my mother.

We would come home on Sundays with all sorts of stories about our dad that I could swear my mother hated. His girlfriend would take us to different places and we'd do different things. It was so funny to see how wrong I was when mom met My, Maddie and D. She was not bothered at all by how we were with them. I was so glad to see that they were getting along because now I could stop feeling like I was wrong for talking about my newest family members and all the things we did together.

The relationship between the entire family has only grown since then and I couldn't be more grateful. Instead of depending on one parent to help me when something's wrong or only having one parent to communicate with, I have three parents. None of them would turn their backs on me and they all listen to what I have to say and are willing to help me get through anything. On top of having three parents that all love and care for me, I now have another little brother that is closer to my age and we are so similar that he actually understands what I'm talking about. We hang out together and it's cool because we have the same ideas about what's fun. Overall I'm extremely thankful for my three parents and everything that comes with them and I'm excited to see what the future will bring to this crazy, loving, blended family.

-TreBill (OB4)

Taylor- 20 yrs old

Divorce sucks for a child no matter what the circumstance might be. The security of having both parents in a home together is gone. Divorce for me was heartbreaking and identity-shattering. I was always aware of my parents' relationship, they had decent days and they had many bad days. Their bad days started behind closed doors and ended in the living room or upstairs where my mother would sleep when it became too much for her to bare. My parents' fights were nerve-wracking because they would start off quiet and erupt into loud shouting or crying. When looking at my parents' marriage it was easy for me to assume that their relationship was the definition of love. It was normal to scream and shout, normal to sleep away from your spouse, normal to throw things when you couldn't express yourself appropriately.

When my parents' marriage was coming to an end I was in middle school. I had just ended a friendship and my parents were dealing with their own problems. I had crushes on the boys in my grade but didn't know how to talk to them. I didn't want the way I talked to boys to turn into what my parents were experiencing. Although I assumed love was supposed to function the way my parents functioned, I wasn't OK with it and it scared me.

My father and I were very close. We were two peas in a pod since I was born. I was an angel sent from heaven and I saved him. I was his first love and no woman had his heart the way I had his heart. My father was always on my side and he never bet against me. He was my Superman and I adored him. All the problems that he and my mother had I figured it had everything to do with my mom. When my parents had enough of each other, my father sat me down. He sat me down in their room and told me we needed to talk. The conversation started simple, then it turned into a conversation where he asked about how I felt about him and my mother. I told him that I noticed all the arguing and that it was getting worse. With tears in his eyes he told me that I was the only woman he ever loved and that he wasn't happy with my mother. I gave him a hug and told him that if he wasn't happy he should leave. He asked me if it was OK if they got a divorce, I looked at him and nodded my head yes. I knew by saying yes my family would be torn apart, but what I didn't know was how quickly. My father thanked me for understanding such a serious situation.

My mother and I were fairly close. In middle school I had the finest mom in the school, all the boys drooled over her pictures that I kept in my locker and all the girls always complimented her. My mother was unlike any mom I knew. She moved when she wanted to move and it was at her pace. My mother said what was on her mind no matter what, she was fearless. She traveled around the world, from New York to the Bahamas. Every few weeks it was a different trip and I always envied her for that. I wanted to be like my mother, I wanted to be a married woman who wasn't tied down to the responsibilities of home. I wanted to travel as far and as long as I pleased because it was an option for me. I wanted children that adored me and supported me the way we adored my mother.

I watched the life leave from my mother's face the day she came home and realized my father was gone. I never had the discussion about divorce with my mother. I didn't think it would matter, because she was going to live her life no matter what. I felt this was my fault. I'd taken my mother's security away. I had taken away her life and I had no way to correct it. I felt as if I had single-handedly broke up my family. I allowed my father to step out of his position within the household without considering the damage it would cause for the rest of us.

I spent the rest of middle school and my freshman year of high school beating myself up every single time my mother wouldn't get out of bed. She wasn't eating, she wasn't talking, she just cried. How could I ruin my mom's life like that? Not only did I ruin it but she did not know that I was the reason behind it all. Did my father ever tell her how I felt and what I said? Or was she blindsided with no idea of my involvement? In my freshman year in high school, my mother asked me if I knew why they got a divorce? I froze in my place and started to tear up. It was in that raw conversation with my mom that I realized it wasn't me and it never was. I wasn't the reason my mother was depressed or the reason my brother was acting out every chance he got. IT WASN'T ME! I went to my room and cried, not only because my mother eased my discomfort and guilt but because my father allowed me to believe that it was me. He didn't place it solely on himself after the conversation where he'd asked for my permission. That was the last we discussed the topic. For a year and a half I had assumed we were partners in fucking up our family. There was no partnership, I placed so much of the responsibility on myself and it was crushing me. The divorce wasn't my fault and even after all these years I still wish he never asked me, would the outcome be different? Probably not, but maybe I wouldn't have been so damaged.

I would like to start by saying I am so proud of who my parents are as individuals and as a pair. Both of my parents traveled down different paths to grow as individuals. I chose not to be part of my father's path back to parenting because I was still angry with him for putting me in that position before the divorce. I watched my mother as she struggled to become whole again. I know my mother's path was hard and nowhere near pretty so I can only imagine what my father's path was like.

If you ever see my parent's interact outside of a romantic relationship you would see that they are dope ass friends. My parents have a cute and corny handshake. They have jokes that go back years. Their vibe is relaxing and watching them makes you wish you had a friendship as dope and deep as theirs. My mother tells me my father has always been her best friend and that trying to be in a marriage for the sake of us got in the way of that friendship.

In the past 5 years I've seen both my parents mature and move beyond their life as a couple. They're a dynamic duo that has no problem going off on any of the kids for getting out of line. They are on one accord, ONE BAND! ONE SOUND! It's really hard to play them against each other because now they want to be friends and talk about EVERYTHING! It feels great to have both of my parents in my life and see that they are both active. Their friendship holds no grudges or resentment from the past because it would get in the way of raising the mini Brady Bunch they have. Time determines everything, it took time for my parents to gain each other's trust, to heal and put the love they have for each other and us back at the center.

-ToTo

Chapter Seven:
Blending the Families

Dub's Story

We have three types of blended families.

First: The Mom has children the new man has no children. We call this King Rising because he has to step into a situation and be more than just the man that is sleeping with mommy. There are several questions needed to be addressed before this family will blend smoothly.

Second: The new woman has no children and the dad has children. We call this the Queen Fallback Position. Her presence is very important however, it must be properly handled by the dad. He sets the tone for the children and his new love. She can do nothing without him because balancing two women is a delicate walk. Good luck, brother!

Third: Both of them have children from a previous relationship. This is THE hardest family to blend because it requires the understanding, maturity, compassion and devotion from up to four adults. This could be hard to manage if you don't know how. We call this The Village.

God has blessed me with several bonus babies, all of them carry a piece of my heart with them and probably don't know it. As with my birth children, there is nothing I would not try to do to make sure they're happy, healthy, safe and prosperous. I love all my babies, even the ones I don't see anymore. I shared with you previously how horrible of a co-parent I was with my first bonus baby, Shorty. I was immature and just wanted to constantly remind his mom of my presence. *Look at me! Look at me!* How desperate and selfish of me, I felt the guilt from that from many years.

Then God gave me Nicco. My husband had impregnated a woman while we were on a break. We talked at length about how this would change the family dynamics and how we would handle outsiders. We had one rule, for everyone. *"If you don't accept this baby and love him the same then fuck you and stay gone until you can."* That was it. That rule applied to parents, grandparents, sisters, brothers, friends, cousins, co-workers, strangers on the side of the road. When you see him, you see us. Point-blank, period. We only lost a few people in our lives because of this rule. For the most part everyone understood and supported what we were doing.

Unfortunately, OB3 was given an ultimatum by his baby mama that forced him to choose between his family with me and the baby. I told him I would leave, I never wanted him to make the choice. He told me, *"No, if I give in to her now I will live my life on my knees for her. She will get over it and we will have our son."* He was right. Eventually, she got a new man or got tired of doing it all by herself, I don't know, but one day OB3 called me on the phone and said, *"Guess who is here?"* It was Nicco. He had a big water head thanks to his dad and a too small pacifier in his mouth thanks to his mom. He was a big three-year-old. Solid and healthy-looking to me, so why is he chewing a pacifier one minute and saying *"Fuck you, bitch!"* the next? I am sure he was coached to say that to me. We actually laughed. It was straight out of the hood baby mama book. Nicco and I hit it off within minutes. It happened like this: I found him outside crying because some kid had his ball, which was not his ball, but that is not the point. I went over to help him. Tears were dried, happiness restored and from that moment we have been good. I never told him to call me mom. I would never ask a child to do something like that. He was three so the concept of who I am was lost on him. All of the other children were calling me mom as he would just grunt or point when he needed something from me. One day, as I was sitting in the car ordering food for everybody, I said, *"Pops, what do you want to eat?"*

He mumbled his order to me which I repeated to the cashier.

"Thank you mommy," he yelled as I passed him his kid's meal.

I smiled. I didn't make it a big deal although my heart was bursting. *"You're welcome, Pops."*

We went through an ugly, but easy custody battle for him when his mom was in jail for domestic assault of her boyfriend. Prior to this arrest, OB3 proposed to Nicco's mom that he come live with us. He noticed he was not doing well in school. He was growing increasingly attached to his siblings and we would have to convince him to leave at the end of the visits. The custody battle cost more than a few dollars and caused more than enough tears. I say ugly because no one wants to fight over a child. I say easy because the case was so strong for joint-custody and was very easy to get considering Nicco's mom's actions. Our lawyer walked in, sat down next to OB3 and I and told us that we could get full custody of Nicco or we could come to a joint-agreement. She had no lawyer, she looked totally blindsided by all of it. My heart was bleeding for her. I took OB3 to the side and begged him not to take her baby from her.

"Dub, you don't know her. She deserves no mercy," he hissed at me. He was pissed at me for being empathetic.

"B, she has been a thorn in my side since our son was born. I know she has made this hard. Look at her. That is her baby too. She deserves mercy."

"We have an opportunity to walk out of here with MY son!"

"Our son."

"We have an opportunity to walk out of here with OUR son. Don't make me compromise."

"We have to. If it is meant to be it will be and we won't be the bad guys. She will. Please. Joint-custody. Please," I pled.

"Fine," he stalked off to tell the lawyer our decision.

Let me explain my decision real quick before I move on. Even though she was a total stalking crazy bitch towards me, that was my son's mother. He loved and adored his mom. She went through rough patches and he didn't notice, he didn't know that he deserved more care and protection. The look on her face that day in court struck me in my heart deeply. I wanted what was best for Nicco but I did not want to take a child from a mom. I knew what it was like to grow up without my mom. Vengeance would have been to cut her head off that day and never look back. Victory would be to keep the parent-and-child relationship intact. Much to OB3's dismay, we chose victory over vengeance. We kept the child first, because that is the most important rule.

Joint-custody worked well for us. Soon we had Nicco consistently attending pre-school, learning new skills and adjusting to being in the house with me and his siblings. He was and still is a very bright young boy that is easily troubled when his environment changes. After a few months, around summer time, his biweekly visits extended to two weeks. It got to the point where he was only going home to his mom on a weekend here or there. I became concerned and asked OB3 to do some investigating to find out why she was not sticking to the arrangements we had set forth in court. It turned out that she was very sick and going through hospitalizations and medication changes. OB3 and I were on rocky ground at this point, but I didn't want our son to be affected by our inevitable divorce.

When B moved out he left me with Nicco and the other kids. Of course, the peanut gallery chimed in.

"I am sorry to hear that. Why did he leave his son?"

"That is so horrible, I thought you guys were forever. Why he leave Pops?"

"You are so strong, but you sure you want to keep Pops?"

Even some of my closest and dearest friends questioned our decision to keep the children together. I actually became hostile in my answer, I was tired of repeating myself. *"That is my son. Period. He left all the children with me. That's it."* Shit!

There was no custody battle for Carmela. Her dad was a no-show the first seven years of her life. On the day she was born, she was maybe a few hours old, and OB3 walked in to hold her.

"Heyyyyy Peanut." He sang to her.

She opened her eyes for the first time hearing his voice. I had mixed emotions. I was grateful that the two of them finally got to meet because I was tired of them playing footsies through my belly. I was extremely sad that her biological dad was not there and did not want to be there. OB3 and I cared for the baby as if nothing had changed. I slipped into deep postpartum depression. I would not hold her, or sing to her or do anything other than make sure she was fed and changed. However, OB3, he would put on T.I. and listen to music and clean up with her hanging from his chest. He talked to her while he played video games. He talked to her like she was the other adult in the house and she would just follow his voice hour after hour. Me, I just sat in a dark room crying, trying to make sense of the heartbreak I felt. How could I have made this decision and put this type of responsibility on OB3?

"Peanut, that is my baby. But you gotta get your ass up and stop moping about this n!%%@. Now. I don't know what it feels like but I know you can get through this like you do everything else."

That is what OB3 told me when Carmela was five weeks old. It was time to go back to work and find a daycare. It was time to return to normal life. We were struggling and I blamed myself for everything. I felt so guilty that OB3 and Peanut were a perfect team and Nicco was off with his mom who was not allowed to see us. I felt so guilty that I spent the first few months of Carmela's life afraid to hold her and bond with her. I looked at her as an extension of pain from her dad and thought if I fell in love with her she would hurt me. OB3, as strong and confident as he was, broke down when he realized I felt that way.

"If you never got anything good from that n!%%@. You got her. Be glad." He told me in his mean ass straightforward OB3 way. He always knew what to say to shake me out of my bullshit.

The same rule applied to Carmela as applied to Nicco. Either accept her or leave us the fuck alone. We were like a Black Avenger's family, we didn't play that shit when it came to our babies. OB3's Grandpa Lou fell in love with her. She was his little ray of sunshine and his face would light up like a Christmas tree when she was around. Oh how he loved our little girl and he was so proud of OB3 for stepping up for her. I couldn't tell who was more protective of Carmela, Grandpa Lou or OB3. One time, my father in law, made some off comment about Carmela not being his grandchild. I expected that from him, he was not the kindest person in the world. OB3 was not having it though. He told his own daddy to fuck off and stay away from his child. His own flesh and blood was cut off over mine.

In the months after OB3 left, we learned that Nicco really did not like to change his environment. The absence of his mom and dad was too much for him so he stopped talking. He did not go mute but he would only communicate with Carmela who would then tell us what he wanted. I knew this was not healthy. I talked it over with OB3 and we both agreed that he should go back home to his mom. I called her up and told her the deal and she picked him up that night. The house felt weird without Nicco there every day.

Carmela was especially lost because they were the closest of anyone in the house. I would still pick him up on weekends and he was back to his normal happy playful self. That made me feel like I had made the best decision for him. A few months later, I get a call from Child Protective Services that Nicco was in their custody because his mom had violated their terms. Apparently, she was not supposed to be in the same home with Nicco and had been reported to CPS for several accusations of abuse. On a surprise visit they discovered Nicco was there and he was taken into custody. I called OB3 to brainstorm because what I was not going to let my baby stay in the system. There was only one big problem, OB3 worked out of the state most of the month. There was no way he could get custody with a work schedule like his. I volunteered to go through the process to get Nicco home and then we would decide later where he would live. I submitted to a drug test. I opened my home up for a home inspection. I had to prove I was financially capable of caring for him. I had to provide letters of recommendation from family and friends.I jumped over so many hurdles I thought I was back in my track days. Eventually, after three agonizing days, Child Protective Services called and told me I could come and pick Nicco up. The look on my baby's face when he saw me on the other side of that door made every hoop I jumped through worth it. He ran to me and jumped in my arms, grinning from ear to ear, *"Hey mama. Where are we going?"* He asked.

"Home baby. Mama is going to take you home with me," I said through tears.

"OK. Is Carmela there?"

"Yeah Nicco, Carmela is waiting on you."

It was the longest drive home because I cried and thanked God the whole way. My emotions were all over the place. When I made the decision to go through with the kinship placement for Nicco, I thought his stay would last for six weeks because that is what Child Protective Services told me. Six weeks and his mom should be out of rehab, her life should be back in order and he could go back to her. Six weeks turned into six months. I declined any payments from the state. He was my child and I didn't need the government to help me take care of him. I went to foster parenting classes. I took him to counseling. I kept him in touch with his mom. Six months turned into a year. At that point, I wasn't sure I'd be able to let him go. We had settled into life again as a family. A year turned into eighteen months. I participated in family meetings with Child Protective Services and the case worker came to visit every month like clockwork. Mom was not doing her part to get him back.

"Are you prepared to get full custody of Nicco if it comes to that?" The case worker casually asked while I was walking her to the front door one day.

"I am prepared to do whatever is asked of me to make sure that Niccos is safe, happy, healthy and whole.", I replied without hesitation.

A few months later, we all stood in court, OB3, baby mama and me. Again. This time the State of Texas was stripping her of her parental rights and giving full custody of Nicco to me. She wailed out in pain, similar to how she did the first time we were in court. This time my heart did not feel a thing. Child Protective Services had given her eighteen months to follow their protocol so that she could get him back. Month after month she had failed. The only way she as going to learn her lesson was if this happened to her.

I pulled her to the side to have a heart-to-heart conversation before the judge called our names.

"Don't take my baby," she kept repeating while crying.

"I am not taking your baby. I will keep him until you are well enough to do it yourself. I would never take your baby away from you." I assured her and I meant that. As a mom, I could not fathom losing my child to the woman that I cheated with her husband to have. Our situation was so complicated.

Once the papers were signed and the emotions were in check, we started a new chapter of our lives. Baby mama and I became very close. We spoke on the phone regularly. She would buy him clothes, underwear, shoes and send them to us. When I was sick, she called to check on me. When I had the new baby she sent clothes for her too. #2 or I would take Nicco to his mom every other Saturday for a visit. The court order stated she was to come to us to visit, but in the spirit of family, I would drop him off to help her out. They talked on the phone several times a week too. The entire time, OB3 was telling me not to do these things. *"Stop jumping through hoops for this broad, Dub. She means you no good,"* he'd warned every time he checked in.

For years, I jumped through hoops for her. I said yes to overnight visits which weren't supposed to happen per the court order. I allowed her to be as much of a mother as she could. Nicco started telling people around me that he was about to go back and live with his mom, repeating information he'd gotten from her directly. Instead of owning up to why he could not live with her, she sold him wolf tickets and it broke my heart to see him waiting for her to come pick him up as promised. She had already missed an important birthday for him, the big 1-0, which we planned together. Then she stopped calling consistently and was showing signs of manic activity. On his last visit to his mom's house, I picked him up and he was sitting on the porch locked out of her house at 9pm in November, in the cold.

"Why are you sitting on the porch, Pops?" I asked, trying to play cool even though I was seething on the inside.

"She won't wake up to open the door for me." He said.

"How do you know she is in there sleeping baby?"

"That's all she did the whole time I was here mama. She would fall asleep at the table, on the couch, anywhere."

"OK, it's cold out here baby. Come get in the car and warm yourself up. You don't have to worry about her she will be fine."

After that, I didn't jump through any more hoops for her. I focused my energy away from being her friend and back on being Nicco's' protector. I told OB3 that she was his baby mama and it was his responsibility to communicate with her from now til forever, I was done being mistreated by her after all I had done. Enough.

Why does Nicco continue to live with you even after OB3 was back in the picture, Dub? I know that's the burning question in a lot of your minds. Simple. We agreed not to break up the siblings. Nicco's connection with Carmela and his other siblings is pretty tight. He loves his dad and visits him often, but there is only one place that he calls home and it is with us.

When I married #2, I gained three beautiful bonus babies. The oldest, Ty, holds a very special place in my heart. She gave me a chance when she didn't have to. She loved me the best she knew how even at times when she was conflicted about how to feel. We had our ups and downs and yet I still love her completely and will always love her. RaiRai, my sassy middle bonus baby, as honest and real as she is with me, she was not feeling me as a bonus mom and that was very hard for me to accept initially. I tried many different ways to reach her but I never really could, because she didn't want that type of relationship with me. I had to learn to respect her boundaries. I respect and honor her for teaching me that I can't win them all. Snickerdoodle, my sweet-as-sugar youngest bonus baby, is the icing on the bonus mom cake. From our first meeting we fell in love with each other. She laughed at my corny jokes. She followed me everywhere I went. She gave the best hugs and the best kisses and she stole my heart. She still has it with her to this day. Even though her dad and I are going through an unpleasant divorce she still texts and calls me to check on me. She was more than just a bonus baby to me, she was one of the good things I got from that marriage. I pray our relationship continues to flourish and that she will never forget how much I love her.

I earned two more bonus babies when OB3 remarried. Demetrius and Madison are a pure joy to be around. My children have spent Christmas with them two years in a row. The babies spent Easter weekend with me recently. They are all my babies. I love them with my whole heart and nothing will change that.

Mrs. OB3 is quite literally the perfect complement to OB3. She makes him better, faster, smarter and more efficient. She has the magic touch and I love it. We are not best friends but we do care for one another. In my illness, she was there for the children without complaint. She didn't expect praise or anything in return. She just loved on them the best she could while their mom was fighting for life. I have thanked her for that in the past, I want to go on record saying *Thank You* again Mrs. OB3. Any time she sees me she always ends the conversation with *"Anytime, Anything."* She means anything I need or anytime I need her she is there. How can I not love and appreciate her? She is the bees knees.

The lesson I've learned is blended families are not easy but they are possible. It takes willing, mature and honest adults to provide a safe environment for the children to open up and flourish. Ladies, if you have a bonus mom in your life who loves your children like you do, show her that you appreciate her. Often. Spread the love, forget the problems you and your ex had. He has made it right by giving the family a great woman and that is love. Appreciate that. He could have picked a trash bonus mom that barely acknowledges your babies. Check your ego and remember to put the children first. If they love her then you are blessed. Don't take that for granted. Menfolk, if your children have a great bonus dad in their lives, show him respect. Thank him for filling in during those times you aren't there. Get to know him. Spend time with him and your children. Foster a bond between them so that they know it is OK to respect and love you and the bonus dad. Ego to the side, it is about what is best for the children. If you have concerns raise them with your ex in a respectful and calm way. Your concerns are valid and should be addressed. Just don't come at your ex on some bogus stuff because he or she has moved on. That is not fair to anybody and will prevent resolutions and progress.

I love my blended family and all of my bonus babies. That is all I have to say about that.

OB3's Story

This 'blending families' shit was a whole new term to me. I didn't understand it. I kept hearing it and would say, *"What the fuck is that? What do you mean, everybody just being cool? Why can't we just say that?"*

Everybody act grown.

Nobody hold any flex against the other.

You don't like your ex so why be mad that they are with somebody new?

Why can't you be around them and be cool?

So what some call 'blended families' is basically everybody being grown and accepting that the ex has moved on and found somebody else. We can all sit in a room and talk, shoot the shit, eat a meal. I don't see the big whoop about what we are doing. This amazing thing that everybody calls it. We were once married, had kids, got divorced, moved on and we can all sit in a room and chill. What is so hard about that?

You have to have common respect for the other people involved. No kissing ass, oh no. Blended families is respecting about respecting all sides. Respect. Simple and plain. Why wouldn't you want to get to know the person your ex is in a relationship with? This person will be around your kids. You need to know them. This is common sense. You don't have to love them. You don't have to call them on the phone and have daily conversations. But a simple, respectful understanding between you and the new guy/girl on the block is all it takes. Just be a grown up about it. You cannot be so childish that you can't have a conversation with a person who is an influence in your child's life. You should want to pick their brain, get to know them a little better. Ego tells you *"Oh nah I can't talk to her, that bitch is that or that n!%%@ is this."* You are supposed to NEED to know who is around your child. Did you forget that the child comes first now, no matter what? Don't rely on some *"She say he cool with the kids"* or *"He says she is good with the kids"* type shit. That is how you end up on the news crying because a *n!%%@* has killed your kid. Of course your ex is going to say their new boo is cool, they're fucking. DUH! What you think they are going to tell you? That is why it is your job to be mature and feel that person out over time, through conversation. If you don't you might end up on the news because you killed a *n!%%@* for fucking with your child and beat up a bitch because she let it happen. Save yourself, hold a conversation. I don't give a fuck if it is ten different people that you have to talk to because the ex keeps switching it up. So what, that is ten important conversations that you must have. I don't give a damn, straight up.

Don't hide your partner from the ex. If he or she will not hold a conversation or your ex will not allow you to simply talk to this person about the weather or sports, then you might want to do some more investigation. There just might be a dirty muthafucka around your kid. Only the guilty try to avoid testifying. I tried to have a conversation or two with #2. He was always on guard. That put me on edge. I had to start asking the kids questions to make sure they were all straight. At first they held it close to the chest. I'm not a patient man but I gave them time to warm up to the idea of talking to me about it. He hated me for real and I had no feelings whatsoever towards him. None. If he hated me, how do you think he felt about my kids? No, fuck that, my sons? I didn't give a damn as long as my children were not being negatively affected, I wished Dub the best.

If you do right by my children you are cool with me. That is what matters. It is about the kids. Your ex could be with somebody who is cheating on her with every piece of tail in the city. That is none of your business, don't run back to your baby mama telling her that shit. Your baby daddy could be with somebody who is the biggest ho from around the way. Again, if it's not about the kids, it's none of your business. Leave that shit be. Only thing that matters is the children. Point. Blank. Period.

The whole point is to get along to set an example. We wanted to show our kids that while we started out wanting to be the American family with two kids, a dog and a white picket fence it didn't work out that way. But, look kids, we can sit in a room together talking and laughing and it is OK, we are still a family, we just added a few members. You never know how two chemicals react until you put them in a beaker together.

How do you think our kids feel about this? They already told you in their chapter, they are happier now than they were when Dub and I were beefing. At family parties or dinners they flow easily between their mom and her significant other and my wife and me. I watch them without them knowing. I watch Dub and my wife off in a corner giggling while the kids run in and out happy to have their parents together even though they are not together. Remember, everything we do is for the kids. Putting them first and ourselves second.

Man listen, I already don't like people. So I am not telling you to be friendly like Carlton from the Fresh Prince of Bellaire. If your ex's significant other gives you a reason to not like him or her you are not obligated to be his best friend. You are obligated to be cordial. If you see him outside of the blended family you don't have to say a word to him if you don't want to. But when your kids are there you say, *"Hi hello. Good day,"* and keep it moving, because it ain't about you. It is for the sake of the kids, the sake of your grandkids. Sacrifice yourself for something bigger than you, for your legacy. Being friends would be ideal but that won't always be possible.

Some of us have grown up in families where just because our mama and daddy didn't get along we grew partial to only side of the family and know nothing about the other side of the family. We were fractured and divided as children. Why? The adults could not blend. They went their separate ways and whoever had the kids got to watch them grow and develop. Trust me. Put that petty ass shit to the side. The relationship is over. Now it is time to give the kids all you got. It's the least you could do.

Another thing, stop talking bad about the ex's significant other. Especially in front of the children. Shut up. If she is ugly or if he is dumb as a box of rocks keep that to yourself. That is so middle school of you to sit up and talk bad about this person with or around your children. It shows you are in your feelings. You still like your baby mama or your baby daddy if you are doing this childish behavior and you cannot tell me otherwise. This information has nothing to do with the children. Who is first? The children. I am going to repeat this until you get the concept.

Last but not least, in order to blend your family you truly have to have patience. You must understand respect and boundaries. You have to understand your new family member their temperament. You have to understand the dynamics of each parent and their personal relationship with the children. It's like a game of double dutch, wait patiently until you see the flow, and then jump in.

Chapter Eight:
The Do's

1. Focus on the children

Dub's Story

This is one of those pieces of advice that seems like a no-brainer. It is so much harder than expected when you are going through a heartbreak, though. Often times, when you are going through a breakup the first thing you focus on is the pain that you feel instead of your children. We shut them out, we don't talk to them about what is happening, we alienate the other parent. It can be so easy to make these mistakes as a relationship is ending. After OB3 announced that he wanted a divorce I was so caught up in my pain. I remember he called one night to check on the kids and I was honest with him.

"B, I don't think I can do this without you." I admitted.

"Yes you can, Dub. You have no choice but to do it."

"But it hurts so much B. Like my heart is breaking in pieces."

"This sucks. I can't imagine how it feels for you. But you

are a mom and you have to fix your face, put on a show, fake it until you make it. You have to do this for the kids."

I did not agree with him but I decided to give it a try after discussing it in family counseling. I began to focus on them being OK. I would assure them that their dad left <u>me</u>, not them. I would encourage them to discuss their feelings and I would address their anxiety and pain without sharing mine. We talked to the children about what was happening and why it was happening on a level that our children could understand. As I began to make it through days without allowing my children to see me in my depths of pain, I began to see a change in them.

"Mama if you want me to be mad at daddy I will." My youngest son, Nicco, said to me one day after he caught me crying in the kitchen.

I bent down to get to his little five year old level and hugged him tight, *"No baby. I don't need you to be mad at dad at all. He is still your dad no matter who he is with he is your daddy forever. Promise me you will remember that."*

"Yes ma'am."

"Now gimme a kiss! That will make my tears go away," I told him. And it did. I wiped away the tears and continued on

with dinner. That was my final lesson in putting the children first. I could not let my pain change the way they saw their dad. I had to work through it and it was hard. OB3 and I stopped bickering eventually. The conversation about why we broke up was silenced and we refocused on the children. We began asking ourselves, *"What do we need to do to make them OK? How can I help them get through this?"*

Placing them first helped us to become better parents despite the fact we were lousy spouses to one another.

OB3's Story

Divorce can be a very trying time for every party involved. Do your best as a human being that has feelings and knows what it is like to have their feelings crushed. Take the time to think *"How is this affecting my children?"* So, you don't love that woman or man anymore. At the end of the day, you must be able to communicate on a respectful level with this person for the sake of the children. No, I am not telling anybody to kiss ass, fuck that! Take them to court if they are expecting you to kiss their asses. Just do your best to take the time to think about your child's wellbeing and how this whole situation is affecting them. At the end of the day, if you can sleep peacefully or if 5-10 years down the line when your child comes and asks you what happened and you can look them in the eyes and tell them why, then you are good. If you cannot, you know that you have fucked up. As a parent, you should do your best to make up for that fuck up. Even if it takes you a lifetime.

2. Come up with an agreement and put it in writing.

Dub's Story

From the day he left our family home to the day we were officially divorced was almost two years. Neither of us was in a big hurry to get it done. In the meantime, we had a written agreement on pick up dates/times and support to be given. It helped to keep us honest with one another. It helped us to check the other one also without the drama of an argument or fight. That agreement also helped us to move quicker towards an uncontested divorce. It helped us to establish our norms as co-parents. It did not require the courts, but if you think that you need the help of the courts, my suggestion would be to file an agreement with the courts. You can spend money on a lawyer, use a pro bono lawyer or file the paperwork yourself. BE FAIR. Don't use this agreement to harm one another or take away rights from the other parent unless it benefits the children. If sending them to dad every other week disrupts them too much then come back to the table and discuss. If the children share a desire to see their dad more than every other weekend then come back to the table. Once agreed upon, put it in writing.

OB3's Story

I did not give a damn about getting a quick divorce. I just wanted my babies and my freedom. Everything else would figure itself out, right? Wrong. I found myself in a position where I had to ask for permission to pick up the children at a certain time or date and that fucked with me. One weekend they would be sitting at home, bored doing nothing. Then the weekend I wanted to get them all of sudden they were busy and had plans. That shit was frustrating. On top of that, they stayed in my pockets. The kids were always calling me for money for lunch, a school project or to go out with friends. Money was no big deal when I was sharing the load with their mom, but as a single man trying to recoup after losing everything it was hard to budget. Dub and I came up with the idea of an informal agreement on money and visitation. It was not set in stone, so we could talk it out if we needed, but for the most part she knew when I was going to pick up the kids and I knew how much money she needed from me every month. It worked out for both of us because we put boundaries in place which didn't require too much talking. When we finally did start paperwork for the divorce that agreement helped as a starting point for us.

3. Honor your word

Dub's Story

Quite naturally, this falls in line with putting everything in writing. It is so important to honor your word when it comes to co-parenting and the children. If you say you are going to pick them up at Friday at 6pm then be there on Friday at 5:59 no excuses. If you say that you are going to pay x amount of dollars on x day have the money. Do not make them ask you for it. Listen fellas, I have zero tolerance with you on this topic. In the eighteen months that OB3 was the primary caregiver I paid him $1,250.00 every month in child support on time every time without excuse. I paid him before I paid my rent, got my hair and nails done, went on any trip, purchased any clothes. My children got my money first and always. Why? My children were my priority and if I was serious about that there was no way I was going to short them so I could go on a trip or ball in the club. He could say I made a lot of mistakes, but keeping my word as the co-parent was never one of them. If I told them that I was picking them up I was there. If he hit a rough patch or needed help and reached out to me then I was there. I honored my word. It is so easy to do when the children are first. We did not aim to hurt one another by using the children. That was beyond childish to us and just would not fly. Many of you mamas are reading this and thinking

"You paid him child support?" The answer to the question is, *"I damn sure did!"* They were still my children. The rules don't change because you are the mother. If I expected his support when I had the children, why would expect a pass from him? Why? Because he is the dad. PLEASE! I told you this journey requires maturity.

OB3's Story

Keeping it one hundred with you this was something I had to work on over time. I lucked up because Dub was an understanding person. I would tell her I was coming to pick up the kids and then hours later after I should have picked them up she would still be waiting. I would get caught up doing whatever I wanted to be doing at the time and that was not fair to her as my co-parent. She had to jump in my ass a few times to get me to understand that if I said I was going to do something I had to do it. I remember one time the children were young because my son was still in diapers. I told Dub I was going to come and get the kids that weekend so she had made plans but I'd forgotten. She tracked me down at my best friend's house, knocked on the door and waited for us to open the door. As soon as she saw my face she walked away leaving the kids there with me. I yelled after her about their clothes or a bag or something. We were in there smoking, drinking and playing video games. It was no place for my kids. She just put her middle finger in the air and got in her car to drive away. I had to pack them up and leave. I called her all kinds of crazy bitches that weekend for dropping my babies off in their pajamas with no clothes or shoes. But she made her point. I was their dad. I was supposed to have those things for them. I was supposed to pick them up when I said I would so that she could have a life and time to herself too. I had to be more than just a dad, I had to be a father and honor my word to her and those children. She still reminds me of this lesson to this day if I fall short. Keep your word fellas. It matters.

4. Everybody PLEASE stay in your lane.

Dub's Story

As I recall, B will have to confirm, I have only formally introduced him to one other man. #2 was around when we were younger so he already knew of him, but I still treated their introduction seriously when we were adults. I have only introduced my children to two men. I was in a serious committed relationship with one, and I married #2, which was the only other man they have ever met. I am very selective with my introductions. I was raised by a single mom and she kept her dating life a complete secret. I am not saying that it was healthy. However, I do believe that introducing your children to every piece you let hit is reckless and this is just my opinion. OB3 has only introduced me to one woman. His wife. They were dating at the time and he sent me a text asking if I was OK with meeting her. The children had already met her and my oldest, Taylor, was very nervous about how we would get along. She loved this woman already after only a few meetings so I knew I had to give her a real chance. I was married at the time to #2 so I wanted it to be something cool like drinks, dinner, bowling or something. Let's just say #2 was never truly into blending us as a family and he blocked it every step of the way if I did not push.

One day, OB3 pulled up to the house and soon-to-be-wife was in the car. Just on the car alone, a cool badass muscle car, I knew she was the ONE. She stepped out of the car and my heart began to race because this was unfamiliar territory for me. I did not know if I would feel jealous or weird. I didn't want to seem too awkward because my sarcasm and dry humor doesn't always register with people. My beautiful confident sister stepped from that car with an afro and this live ass black power shirt and I fell in love! I cannot front. Her smile was easy, she was radiating beauty, and she made him smile. She didn't look us upside the head when OB3 and I did our handshake. My children were hugging on her like she was the second coming. I was impressed from the word GO! I totally understood why he picked her as the first woman to ever introduce to me. She met all of the criteria for a wife and bonus mom. I said a silent *Thank You God* to the heavens. OB3 finally had a helpmate, things might be on the upswing!

While standing right there in the back yard, I sent him a text, *"Don't fuck this up. I am not playing with you."*

"I'm not. I promise." He replied.

We both laughed a genuine laugh as we all hugged and said our goodbyes.

I get it. Not all introductions will go as smoothly as ours did. Every woman he introduces to you and the children might not give you the warm and fuzzies. But, kids first. This is not about you or him. Is this person good to your child(ren)? Does he or she treat them with genuine concern? Watch the children. Give them the space to speak honestly about the new person. This does not mean give them the third degree. Speak nicely of the person and watch how the child reacts. If it is a bad apple the child will let you know. If something is not quite right they will give you hints. However, if you interrogate them they are just going to give you the answer you want to hear in order to protect YOU. You are supposed to protect them, so why put them in a position where they will be protecting you? Think about this too, if you act a fool every time he introduces you to someone he is interested in who will be around the children, he will stop. You lose all control over having a say in who is around your children. The children will hide it, he will hide it. There will be a lot of secrets and lost opportunity to put the children first. You will be stuck getting to know her through a fake page on Facebook or Instagram. How pathetic is that?

Another agreement that we always made to one another, is that we would stay in our respective lanes. I am the Mom, nobody can ever take that title from me no matter how wonderful she might be. OB3 is Dad and nobody could ever be Dad like him no matter what they try to do. OB3 and I knew this and were solid in this fact. Our lanes were defined. We stayed within them. OB3 could not tell me what to do in my personal life that did not pertain to the children and vice versa. I cannot go to OB3 and ask him to do something with the children without expecting him to discuss it with his wife. OB3, by nature, pushes the boundaries and he has done it a few times with me. Each time, I push back and get him on track. I am most proud of us for doing that right. It takes time, work and patience to figure these kinds of things out. It is an ongoing conversation that does not die. Stay in your lane.

OB3's Story

OK, I know some of you are going to say this is some extreme shit, but blending our family means we can take family vacations together. We have one planned for this upcoming summer. Blending families mean we are all present at the children's birthday parties. There is no need to have separate parties. If you and your ex are doing this maturely and with respect, both sides of the family will follow along if they want to stick around. Our children don't have to play mediator and make sure every parent is OK. We have done graduation parties, going away dinners, birthday parties, holidays together as a blended family. Everybody stays in their lane and we all get to enjoy the laughter of our children together. Ask yourself this before you step outside of your lane. *What are you trying to prove? Why are you pushing boundaries? Do you understand your lane?* You should have nothing to prove. Nothing. We blended our families by making sure everybody knew their position.

Your ex does **not** have rank over your significant other. That does not mean you put your significant other on a pedestal and push it down your ex's throat to make a point either. Know your position and play it to perfection. The mama and daddy is the mama and daddy and their positions are already solidified. If daddy is jealous or has a quick temper then he is the weakest link and blending a family probably wouldn't work for that family. If mama is bitter and refuses to let go of her hurt then you probably can't blend that family. Anything can happen, you can always try. But pay attention to the weakest link and get them in their proper positions. If daddy hasn't paid child support in over a year then how the fuck he gonna bring somebody to the children's birthday party? He is tripping and trying to start shit. If mama is calling daddy's phone at 2am on some bullshit, then how the fuck is she going to bring your new bae on a family vacation?

If the significant other feels disrespected or an issue arises, then let mom or dad take it to their ex directly. Let the mom and dad work it out first. Do not be the one to pop off at a party and ruin the whole thing over a side eye or a missed picture. There are proper channels. Do not jump rank. That will get you fucked up. You have to go through the pecking order. If everybody understands this it could be so simple. If you communicate as adults, ***using your words***, everybody can sit in a room and work it out as civil, mature adults for the sake of the children. Do you see how easy this could be? No misunderstanding, nothing lost in translation because everybody stayed in their lane.

5. Stay on the same page with discipline.

Dub's Story

I know a lot of moms that only call the dad to talk when the child is misbehaving. She looks to him for discipline, and that is fine.

"Keep it up, I am gonna call your daddy." She threatens when the child misbehaves.

However, the lesson taught to the child is that Dad is only here to punish me and mom is not going to do anything. This is the fastest way to lose respect from your child. As co-parents, share the good and the bad with each other. If one kid has a great week at school I shoot Dad a text and let him know. If tutoring is needed, and Dad is stronger in the subject I call Dad. If one of them gets an F on the report card, I get Dad involved too. He is not there to just be the belt or the discipline. Let him bask in the glory of the good things too. It is about the children first, right?

Few months ago, my oldest son was getting out of control. He had several reasons. One, he was watching me physically and emotionally deteriorate from my relationship. Two, he was a young, hormone-filled boy that had only one thing on his mind and it was not school. Three, he really wanted to go live with his dad to see what it was like. OB3 and I were in communication back and forth about his behavior and the possibility of him coming to live with him. Our agreement was that he would make it through the school year and then go live with his dad. I really did not want him to go and my reasons were totally selfish. I would miss him. However, #2, at the time, was checked all the way out and he had no real male figure to turn to on a daily basis. I knew I had to surrender my son to his dad, in a rites of passage type arrangement. I would cry as he was packing up his room. I would tear up when he passed me in the hallway. Even after #2 left I still had to go through with the arrangements to let him go with his dad. I had to show him that I was serious and his dad had to show him that he could not run over me. This was a tough time for me. Watching him pack up his things to leave on the last day of school broke my heart. I had to follow through with it. I am glad that I did. Sometimes, a boy needs his dad to get him in line. If you have a dad that is active in his child's life let him be more than just the hammer.

Discipline is for the benefit of the children and should be supported by all parents. It should be respected by both homes as well. If the kid is on punishment at Mom's house, inform Dad and let him extend the punishment in his home. Please, whatever you do, continue to discipline during and after the divorce. Do not let the children see that they can use the divorce as a reason to have poor behavior. Maintain your same standards and beliefs for the children that you had when in the home with them. This is vital.

OB3 violated this rule once and we had to have a serious talk. Check it, our boy Nicco was doing the damn fool in school with his grades. At this time, #2 had a set of broken ribs so he was not in the best shape. I was always tired and fatigued, plus there was nothing that I could say that could get through to Nicco. As I stated earlier, I kept OB3 up to date with the good and bad actions of our children. I thought it would be good for Nicco to see us as a united front on his behavior and grades, so I asked #2 if OB3 could come to the house and talk it out with us and Nicco. #2 agreed and OB3 and I setup the time and date. It was around 8:00 pm and I was standing in the kitchen getting dinner ready. OB3 walked in with a belt around his neck. I think he spoke to us but I can't remember. The next thing I knew, OB3 was in full daddy mode with Nicco. He was going off on him while spanking him. #2 got up in pain to see what was going on. He looked at me like, *"What the fuck you letting go on in here?"* It happened so fast I could not move to stop it. I could NOT believe OB3 walked into this man's house without speaking and commenced to beating our son's ass. It was not so much that he didn't have the right to discipline his own son, it was more so that he didn't go through with the plan we had discussed. It made me look like I had set it up that way and I did not. #2 talked about that night for months before he left me. He was pissed and rightfully so. OB3 and I talked about it and he understood and apologized for any disrespect. That is when we came up with the plan that next time he wanted to discipline any of the children in that manner, he would just pick them up and take them with him.

OB3's Story

Dub's husband (at the time) was tripping because I walked in their house and laid down my law with our son. I didn't think I was doing anything wrong, but I could see how it looked. I apologized for bringing the heat down on her, that was never my intention. I guess my first piece of advice is to respect the other parent's home. Dub and I have very different methods for discipline. In her young tender days we had the same, but now she has gotten old and soft. Dub likes to talk to the children and get a clear understanding. I don't do all that talking shit. They only have one job. Go to school, make good grades and behave. What's so hard about that? If you ask me, nothing! I do not give an inch. I have learned to stop reacting immediately and to discuss the game plan with Dub first. That is all it takes really, communication. The goal is to make sure the children are not playing the parents against each other because they will. Trust me. If you let them have an inch during the divorce they will act like they run the whole show. Not me. No sir.

Personally, I look at it like this, as a man in the home with my bonus babies, I have the right to discipline them. I provide for them as my own so I discipline them as my own. If your children are living under the roof with another man this is something that you need to discuss so everybody is on the same page. I am sure there are some people who don't think the bonus parent should do any of the disciplining. I respect that, not everybody can handle such a responsibility. Communication, respectful and honest communication, can solve any discrepancies with this. Just be a united front when it comes to the children, all of the adults stick together even if you disagree behind doors.

Chapter Nine:
The Dont's

1. Stop fucking

Dub's Story

This may seem like an obvious piece of advice but you'd be surprised how many co-parents break this rule. It is easy to fall into the routine of having sex with your ex after the anger subsides. Say he comes over to drop off the kids and you answer the door in his favorite tights. You smell like fresh rose water and jasmine. Music is playing in the background and you've just been enjoying a nice glass of wine. You are relaxed and he sees that all over your face. It reminds him of the good old times when it was fun and light between the two of you. He stays a little longer to put the kids to bed and joins you for a glass of wine once they fall asleep. One thing leads to another and you are fucking.

Stop it!

There are several reasons why having sex is not a good idea for you as co-parents. First, the promise is to keep the children in first place. Having sex with your ex means he or she will be around more and that will give the children a false impression which may lead to false expectations. My ex and I broke up five times before we finally divorced. Five times the children had to watch us go from non-speaking terms to inside jokes and extended visits. Overnight stays, extra time at dinner, outings together as a family even though we were not a couple, all of this confusion because I was still giving the cookies to their dad whenever he called. If he had a girlfriend, or if I had a boyfriend, we might reduce the amount of times that we hooked up, but it didn't completely end until the final breakup. We both made the mature decision to remove the sex from the co-parenting contract and that is when we began to really work together as a team. The kids were clear on the terms of our friendship. The tension was removed when we were in each other's presence and the children became the number one priority again. Don't get me wrong, it was tempting sometimes. Just remind yourself that he is an ex for a reason and your babies need you to do this one solid for them. You can do it girl. Stop fucking him.

Another reason it is so important to stop hooking up with your co-parent is that you cannot move on emotionally or physically if you are still dipping in the pot. I remember during one of our breakups, I was really feeling this guy who I'd started dating. He was so romantic and kind, smelled like soap and money. He would surprise me every Friday with gifts, big and small. He really made me laugh. The only thing preventing the relationship from moving forward was that I was still creeping to my ex after the kids were asleep. I had a birthday party and this guy spent a lot of money to make sure that everyone at my party was well fed and drunk. My ex, being the suave ass dude that he can be, showed up to the party looking like new money. He had on a blazer, tan suede that smelled like a new baby calf, paired with fitted pants and grown man shoes. Not polo boots from 1994 or Timberlands or Jordans. No, he had on a classy brown pair of leather loafers. I was wet on the spot! I had never seen him dressed up for anything, let alone dressed up for me. The guy I was dating noticed a change in my demeanor and he worked harder to get my attention. He lavished me with more Patrón shots, more flattery and more cash-money pinned to my shirt. He could have given me the keys to a Bentley and I would not have noticed because my ex was sitting less than ten feet away from me looking like my perfect picture of a man. If I would have closed my eyes and made a wish he would look, smell and walk exactly as my ex was at that moment. Why didn't he do that shit when we were together?

Asshole.

The party ended and it is time to go home. Decisions, decisions. Who would I go home with? The man that had courted me like a perfect gentleman for over two months? Or, my ex who was standing there looking like my favorite candy, Sugar Daddy. The mind and body are connected when you are constantly having sex with someone. I knew that logically-speaking I should go home with the nice guy. However, my body knew the feel, smell and taste of my ex. The familiarity of his touch was way more enticing than the exploration of some stranger. We walked out of the club, the cool brisk air sobered me up a bit and we began to talk. He apologized for making my friend feel uncomfortable but he just wanted to talk to me. He needed me to hear him out and I had a few things to get off my chest as well. So I bid farewell to the nice man and my ex and I went back to my place to hear each other out. Funny thing is, we did not have sex that day. We talked until the sun came up about nothing and everything. The level of intimacy we shared that night without touching one another was so rare that I did not want it end. I thought I didn't need to find a man because I had a piece of man right at my fingertips at all times.

Stop sexing so you can move on, sis. Trust me. That nice guy married the next woman he dated after me. He moved her to a beautiful home in the suburbs, gave her a cute car and two beautiful children. He adores and loves that woman to this day because he really was a great guy with a big heart. That could have been me posted up in the 'burbs hosting dinner parties. Stop fucking. Seriously.

My very last reason for telling you to stop giving up the booty is that your ex thinks because he is still having sex with you he can still control you. The agreements that you make with him about the kids go to the wayside when he has a change of plans.

In a non-sexual co-parenting situation this is addressed without emotion. But when he is hitting that and you try to hold him to his part of the agreement he will say you are acting crazy or you are just mad because he is going out with his friends or you are just jealous. You know that none of this is true but you are having sex with him so how can you come at him without that being part of the discussion? When he does move on, instead of getting to know his new woman for the sake of the children, you will be too busy finding flaws, acting stank and behaving like a typical ex. That is not a good look. The kids are supposed to be the priority, not the dick. Focus ma. You can do this. Stop fucking him.

OK I know I said the last point was my last reason, but I have to add this bonus reason. Friends do not fuck. The entire purpose of co-parenting is to show your children that they have both parents in their lives even if you two are no longer a couple. They watch the two of you speak positively of the other, have easy conversations, laugh, discipline them on the same accord and communicate about them. Children know that mom and dad are on the same page and that they cannot divide and conquer the two to get what they are want. That is what a friendship will provide to your children. Those are amazing benefits. It does not mean that you have to be his best friend but having a friendship is vital to the children's wellbeing. You cannot be his friend while busting it wide open for him. That chapter of your lives has ended. Like a bad weave, it's time to let it go.

OB3's Story

In order to blend the family, you must be totally detached and void of any deep emotions toward your ex. In my opinion, this is the major factor that stops people from being successful at blending families. I can be around Dub and her significant other and watch them hug or kiss and think, *"Aw that is cute."* I am detached. She can see my wife play in my hair or fix my clothes and think, *"That is so sweet."* She is detached. You have to move on and be happy that your ex found someone who can put a smile on their face. That is the mother or father of your children. If they are happy, the kids are happy. If the kids are happy then you are doing something right. If you cannot be happy for your ex you are a selfish fuck.

Dub and I broke up so many times over our near 20-year on again, off again relationship and we would hate each other's guts but still hook up. I would do my best not to spend the night because we didn't want to confuse the kids. Familiar pussy is good during a drought or when you're still sorting out your feelings, but it is not good when you are attempting to co-parent. It messes with your head. She was dating a whole dude and here I was coming over like a thief in the night to get some ass. Just because she is your baby mama does not mean you can have the cookies for the rest of your life. That is an urban legend patna. It can also be a trap. You know women use sex as a way to confuse and deflect, and it works because the sex is good. Don't get caught up in that. Just stop fucking altogether. In our final breakup, we had one last ride and then sex was never spoken of again. Stop fucking, it turns black and white to grey.

2. Don't use the courts as a first resort

Dub's Story

It is ironic that as I am writing this book, I am currently going through a custody battle with #2 over our two daughters. I thought that we were great friends. We had a long history, almost eleven years of just being friends with no romantic connection. My head and my heart were in constant war over my relationship with this man. This is why we are in court. My heart wants to give him whatever he asks for but my head knows that I am responsible for our children and I have to protect them because he will not. My advice to you is if you can avoid the court system at all costs when it comes to your family, please do. It should not take a piece of paper signed by a judge to get financial and emotional stability from the other parent. Sometimes emotions get in the way of making the best decisions for our children. I am human, I can admit that. I was deeply wounded by the breakup especially because it took place during one of the scariest times in my life. As a non-confrontational personal I avoided any arguments regarding the children with #2. I did not ask for any financial support. I did not initially deny visitation. I waited patiently for the divorce paperwork to be served and yet it never came. As time passed and he began to bully me, I eventually had to stand up for myself and my children. Allowing him to treat me badly was my choice, allowing him to do the same to our daughters was not an option. Co-parenting effectively with him, thus far, has not been a viable option. As a result, we have found ourselves entangled in court. Truth is every breakup does not end happily ever after with the parents and step parents being best friends.

OB3 and I were two willing parents. Before our first born took her first breath we promised to put her first no matter what happened to us as a couple. It was not an easy promise to keep sometimes. There were times when OB3 did not support the children financially. There were times when he was absent for long period of times. There were times when he would break his agreements with me so that he could hang out with his friends or some new flavor of the week. There were times when I was so overwhelmed with parenting that I moved out and left the children to live with him full-time. There were times when I would call him for help and he would be there no matter how trivial.

One time, I lay in bed in agonizing pain after a double root canal. I had no money for my pain medications or soup to make me feel better. The children were in the living room watching television and Taylor tried to make sandwiches for their dinner. The phone rang a few times but in my pain I didn't want to answer. It was their father calling for his nightly chat with the children. He hung up and called right back. This time I answered because I knew that if he had to call again he was on his way to our home.

"*Hello,*" I answered weakly.

"*Dub? What's wrong? You sound like somebody killed your dog,*" OB3 said.

"*I'm OK, B.*"

"*Don't lie to me. What is wrong with you? Where are the kids?*"

"*I just had some dental work today and I don't feel too good. They are in the living room watching TV.*"

"*Let me talk to Taylor,*" he said.

"*Taylorrrrrrrrrrr your daddy is on the phone,*" I whimpered.

She took the phone and walked away to have a private conversation. She returned with the phone and placed it next to my bed before turning off the lights and closing the door. "*Mama, Daddy said he is on his way,*" Taylor informed me before finally closing the door.

I exhaled a breath of relief and fell into a pained slumber. After what felt like hours of sleep, I woke up to the moon shining through my bedroom window and my favorite blanket spread across my feet. I struggled to sit up in bed but the pain in my mouth traveled to my head and I let out a loud *"Owww!"* OB3 opened the bedroom door to see what was wrong.

"Dub you are back in the land of the living! Are you ok?" He asked with concern.

"I am in a lot of pain B. How long have you been here?" I asked.

"Take your pain meds. The kids are fine. I brought them some food, made sure they took a bath and I'll get them in bed before I go. I can lock the bottom lock so no one disturbs you," he said. He had it all planned out. The kids were going to be fine. It was me that was a mess.

"I don't have any pain meds."

"Why not?"

"I don't have the money for them so I left them at the pharmacy."

"Dub, which pharmacy?"

"The one on the corner by the chicken joint."

OB3 walked out of the door mumbling something under his breath. I slumped back down in the bed and tried to find a comfortable position to rest in. As I lay there in the bed, tears spilled from my eyes. I was grateful to my ex for rushing over to take care of the children without any question. It is tough being a single mom sometimes, especially times when I was in pain and couldn't do much for them. The tears were hot and salty as they fell from my eyes on to my lips. I didn't know if the tears were from the pain or from my gratitude towards my ex who treated me as a real friend would. Time passed, maybe fifteen minutes or so and OB3 walked back into my room and turned on my light. He started pulling stuff from a plastic bag. A gatorade, pill bottles and chicken soup with rice because he knew I hated chicken noodle soup.

"Dub, get up. Take these pain meds, they will help. The pharmacist also said you need to start these antibiotics right away so the swelling will go down." He was barking orders at me while passing me the fluids and the medication. *"Don't worry about the soup, I am warming some up. You have to put something in your stomach."*

That's when I knew that the tears were from gratitude. We were horrible partners in marriage but somehow we were great friends when apart. He knew that if I was down and sick I could not take care of the kids. So he had to make sure I got back on my feet so he would know that his children were taken care of properly. It was for this reason I never felt the need to drag him down to court and make a judge tell him what he had to do to be a dad. In the State of Texas, in a divorce decree, child support and insurance are two things that are required to be defined and ordered. At the time of our divorce, he could afford the payments that were set in the divorce. Some years later he lost his job and couldn't pay. I did not call the Office of the Attorney General to report him every month like some women do. I didn't text or call him incessantly asking him for money that I knew he did not have. Even after he got on his feet and got it together I still did not press him on child support or visitation. The court order was just a guide for us. It was an outline in the event we ran into trouble with our communication. However, OB3 and I prided ourselves on having our own code of conduct when it came to our children. Any time I wanted to take his head off because he was out there balling and I was barely paying the bills, I reminded myself of the days when my friend made sure that I was well enough to take care of our children.

Many years later, when our children were in the teen years, OB3 came to me and asked me to remove the child support order from him. It was being reported on his credit and it was hindering him from moving forward. He promised that if I took the support order away he would still provide support in any way, all I had to do was ask. He owed me a fine automobile in backpay for child support, a Mercedes E-Class or a BMW, a nice sum of change was owed. Yet, I saw him trying to get himself together. I heard him when he apologized for his absence. I knew the courts were not where we belonged. After a lot of deliberation and meditation, I removed him from court-ordered child support. It felt liberating to me. I was able to take the matters of our children into my own hands and remove the third-person that did not know us or understand us. It was my olive branch offering to OB3 that, if he honored his promise to me, I would honor my promise to him again and take care of these children the best way we knew how.

Years later, as I was going through my second divorce and preparing to undergo a bone marrow transplant, it was OB3 who took care of things for me financially making sure the children were OK. When the AC was broken, he paid to repair it. He made sure there were groceries were in the house, the light bill was paid, the WiFi remained on and he did all of this without question for all of my children, not just the children that belonged to him. He called me one day while I lay in recovery after a surgery and those same tears of gratitude fell from my eyes as I thanked him for making sure I was ok so I could take care of our children. No court could order that type of support.

This is why it is so important to think very carefully before rushing to file child support or modify custody and visitation. The decision should not be made while emotional. If you are fresh out of the relationship and find out he has another girlfriend, pause.

Do not file yet. Give him the opportunity to be a father without being forced before you involve the judge and courts. Trust me on this sis. Take a deep breath and think before you do anything that could permanently damage the co-parenting relationship. It does not matter if you have a new man who can take care of you now. It does not matter if you hate his guts and wish he would die. All that matters now is what is best for the children. Give him time to figure out what kind of dad he wants to be now that the relationship with you is no longer the same.

Remember how OB3 and I both had outside babies around the same time? When my daughter was born, I was a complete emotional nutcase. My hormones were raging. I was so angry with her father about the way he was denying her. My head and heart were seething with anger and I wanted to do something to get back at him so badly. Child support was the only thing I could think to do that would hurt him because he loved money so much. One day I was sitting at the computer, completing the child support application when OB3 walked in and saw me. He closed the laptop and said, *"No. Give that man some time to figure it out. If you do this now he will always have it as an excuse. Just go to him, tell him how much you need and come to an agreement. If he violates the agreement and you are no longer mad then you can go to 'the man' for help."* I could not understand how he was compassionate towards the man that I'd a baby with and who was clearly not going to be present. However, I listened to his advice and did not file child support on him on that day. I contacted #2 and we came to the agreement of $100 per week which I would pick up from him every Friday at his job. It went well for the first few months. He paid on time without any real issues. Then I started having to wait an hour for him before he would show up, or he would come with $60 instead of $100 as agreed. Or he would want a kiss and some attention before he would pay. This went on for months. The last time I went to get support from him, I came home and I told OB3 that I was done begging him to care for his child.

He asked me, *"Are you angry?"*

"No, B, I am just tired," I responded.

"OK. You gave him a chance. He forced your hand. No one can say you didn't try because I watched you jump through hoops to try."

That is the difference between willingness and being forced to do. Some men attach ownership to you because of the child and will treat the child poorly because he is no longer into you. Those are the brothers that you take to court. But the good guys who show up without question, honor you as the mother of their child, never take advantage and help however they can are the men you give a chance. Figure out which one you have before you involve the courts.

OB3's Story

I have said this before and I will go on record saying it again, I could not have picked a better mother for my children. Dub is bat shit crazy, anybody that knows her knows that. But Dub is always calm and fair. Even in situations when I could not be, she is. The courts were not a huge factor in our relationship. One time, 15 years ago, she got mad because I was tripping and filled out the child support application, but she never followed up with it. We hired a lawyer and went to court to gain custody of Nicco. That was about it. While we were going through the divorce, she asked me how much I could afford to pay in child support. She knew I was starting over and didn't want to drag me over the fucking coals. I told her I did not care but she kept asking. I think the judge ended up selecting the amount when we got divorced.

I paid it without hesitation while I was working full-time at my gig on the oil rig. I was happy to send her the money, as long as the children were straight I could be OK. Then I lost my job and stopped paying. I don't know if you know this but child support hits a man in a bunch of ways. The interest is added every day. It is reported on your credit report. You can't renew your license or your vehicle registration. If your baby mama calls enough times they will even lock your ass up in a cage. Which is dumb because how the fuck I am supposed to make money in jail? Anyway, the amount of money I owed Dub started stacking up. I was trying to get back on my feet after being unemployed so I just went to Dub and asked her to take me off of child support. She had every right to say no, I would not have been shocked if she had. My homie did not tell me no. She told me she had to talk it over with her husband and would get back to me. Months passed and I heard nothing about it. One day out the blue she texted me to tell me the case had been closed and back pay had been erased. I was happier than a kid in a candy store and I promised her that if the children needed anything to hit me and I would do my best to get it done.

There were times I could not help out financially. She did not trip. She didn't threaten me with the courts. Our view of the courts were sour. I felt like I didn't need some judge to tell me how to pay for my children or when I could see them. We have never stuck to a real visitation schedule. If she ever needs a break she reaches out to me. If I am in town and want to see them I just shoot her a text and it is cool. It's sad but it's true that some people need that court paper in order to act right. Dub could have shut the door on me and my back-and-forth shenanigans long ago but she didn't.

Before I go, let me say this, when I was locked up Dub and I read the book Art of War together. Dub used the *"Pick battles big enough to matter, small enough to win"* rule. Now that I am older and have more experience I choose my battles based on the best outcome. Small victories add up. Don't run to the courts for every little thing, learn how to compromise and work it out without needing a judge to tell you what to do for your children.

3. DO NOT (this is all caps because this is important) COMMUNICATE THROUGH THE CHILDREN

Dub's Story

I do not care how old the children are at the time of the breakup. Keep them out of grown folk business. Visitation, child support, changes to schedules, medical emergencies, school performance and anything else you can think of, related directly to the children should not be relayed as messages through the children. They hate it. They don't want to do it. They don't want to deal with your piss poor attitude or messed up reaction. They don't want to be quizzed on details because all they have is the message. Do not make them the messenger. They are children. They didn't break up - the two of you did. Stop it.

OB3 and I made this mistake during the time between our final separation and divorce. Our children were 13, 11, 6 and 6. The oldest even had her own cell phone at the time. (Cell phones and kids were not as popular as they are at this time). If OB3 was on his way to pick up the children, he would call our oldest. If he was going to be late, he would call our oldest. If he didn't deposit my money into my account on time, I would send our oldest to ask him for my 'package'. If the children needed something, I would tell my oldest to call and tell her dad. As parents, we thought we were doing great. Things got done. We didn't have to speak. It was a win-win. However, my oldest was suffering from it tremendously. She began to lose her hair from pulling at it so much. She was becoming withdrawn and losing friends. She was overwhelmed with the burden of being the pigeon messenger between the two of us. She admitted this to me in family counseling one day. Like a ton of bricks falling on my heart I wept in shame. I never thought about how it made our children feel to see that we could not even hold a cordial conversation with each other. It was so stupid because during this time we were not arguing or having any issues with one another. We were just no longer a couple.

One time, the children came home so excited about their dad getting a dog. *"Mama, Daddy is going to get a pit bull, that is my Christmas gift!!!"* my oldest exclaimed.

"Did you give him the same Christmas list that you gave me?" I asked with an attitude.

"No. He didn't ask." She responded.

"Just so I am clear, you gave me list with an iphone, laptop, and new wardrobe on it. But you jumping up and down because your daddy bought a funky ass dog?" Now it was time to drill down.

"Well you know I am scared of dogs, so this was not my idea," My son chimed in.

"Since this dog is obviously the best present you could get, I will just save my money and buy the dog food." I said as I walked off.

I was pissed. I could not believe they were letting him get away with a dog that was FOR HIM as a Christmas gift for them while I was going into debt trying to fulfill their Christmas wish lists. Enough was enough, it was time for us to open those lines of communication back up. Once I removed the children from our lines of communication, OB3 and I learned something very important. The kids were getting over on us. The Divorce Curse is what it is called. They knew that we were not talking to one another so they would ask OB3 for something I had already said no to and get it. They would get in trouble at home and be on punishment, but would not tell their dad so they were free as birds on their weekend with him. They would make me feel bad about not having something that they had at their dad's house so I would go out and buy it. These kids were good at the playing the Divorce Curse card. Once we began to talk on a regular the children began to realize that we were on the same team and The Divorce Curse was broken.

OB3's Story

Yeah, so this is another one of the rules that I really fucked up with in the beginning. My stance was my children were old enough to talk so why did I need to talk to their mama? I did not have a problem with Dub, I just did not see the point in speaking directly to her. It was a big problem. I only got half the story when I was talking to the children only. I did not know that my son was fucking up in school when I was buying him video games at my house. I did not know that my daughter was fucking off her money on her friends and not herself when I was transferring money to her account every time she called. It took Dub calling me and explaining that she was not trying to be in my business but we needed to talk for me to understand how important it was to stop sending messages through our children.

My son, he was always trying to make every situation work out in his best interest no matter how many other parties are involved. I would call him and set up arrangements to pick them up for the weekend and Dub would know nothing about it. It only took a few times doing that before I said *"Nah son, you not gone keep making me look foolish."*

These kids were getting over on me big time. They would ask their mother for some shoes or something and her answer would be no. Her reasons were sound, you are not doing your chores, grades aren't right, etc but do you think they told me any of this? No. Of course not. They'd come home flossing new shit and Dub would be ready to slit my stupid ass throat because I was undermining her every move as a parent.

Learn to talk to each other directly as parents. Keep the children out of the middle of the message. It keeps down confusion. It sets boundaries. It keeps both sides informed. It helps with long-term decisions. It saves money. It saves time. Kids don't know shit. Just talk to each other. If you could have sex to make a baby you can talk. Text, email, smoke signal whatever it takes, just keep the kids out of the middle of it. Please and thank you.

4. Do not force the children to choose a side.

Dub's Story

In the Bible, King Solomon saw two women fighting over the same child and ordered to cut the baby in half so they could both have a piece of the child. The true mother of the child begged the King not to cut the baby in half, just give her to the other mom. King Solomon ruled that she was the true mother because she loved the child too much to see any harm come to him even though she would lose and be hurt. When you ask for the children to choose sides, you are basically cutting the baby in half. Think about it. Your child is 50% your DNA and 50% his DNA. By asking your child to select a side, you are unquestionably asking that child to remove one half of themselves. How do you love that child and ask them to do this? Ask yourself that question. Why would you ask your child to love and care for one parent more than the other? What a burden to lay on the shoulders of a child. If they are in emotional or physical danger, I understand removing that danger from their lives. On the other hand, if you just don't like your ex because they're a jerk towards you or they hurt you and you are mad, don't involve your child in your petty emotions.

Before OB3 told me he wanted to get a divorce, he went to talk to our oldest daughter about it. He explained to her that we were not getting along because I did not like him always going out with his friends. This was a partial truth but still too much information for a 13-year-old to process properly. After consideration, she told him it was ok to divorce me because that was not fair and she wanted to see him happy. Fast forward one night after family counseling our oldest daughter was having a nervous breakdown about something and I didn't know what to do, so I grabbed her and told her.

"Talk to mama, what is wrong baby?"

"If I tell you then you will be so mad at me!' She stated.

"There is nothing you can tell me that will make me stop loving you, even if I do get mad."

"You don't understand it was really bad mama!"

"Talk to me, please baby, tell me."

"The divorce is all of my fault. He asked me if I would be OK with it and I said yes. I am so sorry!"

The words stung. Not because she told him that she was OK with it but mostly because my baby was carrying around guilt that was not hers to carry! Anger began to swell up inside of me, I felt hot around the neck and ears and the shaking started. With tears in my eyes, I forced her chin up so that we were eye-to -eye and said, *"I am so sorry that you have carried around this guilt this long. Believe these words like they came from God himself: this divorce had nothing to do with you. Nothing. It would have ended whether you said yes or no. I am so sorry that you were placed in such an awful position."* And we held each other and cried until the tears dried.

Oversharing and asking children to take sides is child abuse. Playing mental games with your children to turn them against the other parent is child abuse. Molesting a child's mind so that they feel the need to protect your broken heart or choose the 'right' side so that you feel better is child abuse. I am serious. Check yourself. Once upon a time you chose that man and a child was born from that decision. You must sit in that decision and accept it. Don't abuse your children emotionally by forcing them to choose sides.

OB3's Story

This a tough one for me because I did this shit and paid dearly for it. Before I pulled the trigger and left Dub I had a talk with Taylor about leaving. She has always been mature for her age and she always wanted me to be happy, so I ran my mouth to her without thinking about the impact the conversation might have on her. I basically asked her if it was OK if I left her mom. She gave me her blessing. We were tight like two peas in a pod so I thought I was just talking something through with her the way I have done since she was knee-high to a duck. It backfired on me though because when I did finally leave her mom some months later Taylor felt like it was her fault because she told me yes.

She sat in that guilt for a long time and stopped talking to me. My daughter. My world. My lifeline. My ace. She refused my calls. She refused any visits with me. She did not pick up the phone to call me. I could not pick up the phone to call her. She blocked me on social media. She basically erased me from her life and that just about took a *n!%%@* out. I went to Dub to fix it and she told me she could not fix it because that was something that I had to work out with Tay. I wrote her a letter trying to pour out my heart and tell her I was sorry. She wrote me back basically saying *fuck your sorry.*

One of my major causes of depression was the breakdown of my relationship with my baby. I blamed her mama. I blamed her for not understanding. Eventually, I had to take a long look in the mirror and realize I did that shit. I made her pick a side and that was too much for a 13-year-old little girl to handle. I had raised her to be tough but that was just wrong and even though I didn't do it on purpose I still did it and I had to make it right. I had to make sure she knew that it was me and not her. I had to get her to let me back in with my actions and not my words. I did everything I could and then I stepped back and let her come to me on her time. She knew too much about our divorce because of me. She saw too much pain and hurt in her mama and she wanted to protect her. She was so mad at me. Thank God again for a mother like Dub because she never helped Taylor hate me. She kept reminding her that I was her dad. I'd made a mistake and I deserved another chance when she was ready to give it. At the end of her senior year she was ready to give me that second chance and I was right there with open arms waiting for her. I fucked up and she forgave me and I will never take advantage of that trust with her again in my life, with her or any of my other children. Don't fuck up and make them pick sides because that side might not be yours.

4. Never speak negatively about the other parent to the children or in their presence.

Dub's Story

Forty-six chromosomes. That is how many chromosomes are present in a human being. Twenty-three come from you and twenty-three come from Dad. That means that when you are speaking negatively about your ex-partner you are tearing apart piece-by-piece 50 percent of your child. Think about that for a moment. He has his daddy's eyes, feet, thinking pattern, hair or whatever. Then you slam his daddy, which he identifies with, and you think that is helping your child to be a happy, well adjusted, healthy child? No. Stop it. NOW. Don't do it when the child is anywhere in your vicinity. Don't do it in the house, don't do it in the car, don't do it in their face. DO NOT DO IT. Why? In my very humble opinion, it is mind molestation. You are molesting that baby with poison about themselves. Just as the innocence is stripped from a child after rape so is their innocence stripped from them when you call the other parent names and sit them in the middle of grown-up pain. There were times where I hated OB3, like deep seated hatred from pain. And #2, I still cannot find a nice thing to say, so I say nothing.

My mama taught me never to tear a man down who is not there to defend themselves. Thank God for texts because when I am really raging I can text my feelings out without the children knowing. However, you can ask all of my children, strap them to a lie detector test and strike me to hell if any of them say *"Mommy said you were stupid or sorry or dumb or whatever."* That's not my place. First, I don't want them to think that half of them is stupid in any kind of way. Second, it is not my place to color the picture of their father for them. If he is stupid, sorry, Dumb or whatever, trust me the truth will come out.

OB3's Story

Fuck. I had to learn a lot as a man and father on this one. My other baby mama, the one we do not speak of, is a complete fuck up. That's the realest shit I can say. Off topic, but not really. Men be real selective with who you're fucking because every one of them is a potential baby mama. I was not thinking about that shit when I was fucking her. She let me move work into her apartment, she always had food and was always down to fuck. Pure convenience is what she was and I ended up with a lifetime commitment with her. It has been so hard not to give my son the real deal on his mama. I have to let Dub handle those conversations because she is the nice one. My wife also works on me because she understands me and knows I hate to be fucking played with. It was also hard for me to keep my tongue about Dub's second husband. I will keep my thoughts to myself but let's just we never saw eye-to-eye, because he could never look me in the eye. Dub loved him and the kids seemed to like him OK, so I did my best to go along and get along. It takes a man to really understand the situation and to hold your tongue when you know another man is talking down on your name.

I won't lie, I had issues with ub letting this happen. I talked to her about it and she was stuck between defending my name and honoring her marriage. That is a hard spot to be in and I felt bad for my homegirl because she had to go through that. I just made it clear that my name needed to be respected in the presence of my children. That was all I could I ask and I think Dub did her best to honor that. In the end, one of the reasons Dub and #2 couldn't work is that he wouldn't honor this simple rule. I wish it could have played out different for her sake. But my stance remains the same, keep my name out yo' mouth.

5. Don't allow significant others to discipline your children without talking about it as co-parents.

Dub's Story

This is not going to be popular amongst the masses. The old school of thought is if he or she is helping to raise the child then he or she should have the right to discipline the child. But, answer these questions:

How many stories have you watched on the news where the stepparent killed a child or molested a child?

What are you going to do if the other co-parent does not want the significant other discipline the child?

Why is the biological parent leaving discipline up to a new person?

What happens if the child claims child abuse?

In order for discipline to be effective, the child must first respect you. If you are not the biological parent, respect has to be established. In order to establish respect, you have to show respect. That means, you have a conversation with the adults and respect the boundaries put in place regarding discipline.

When I was married to #2 we had a rule that each of our children had to clean the kitchen for a week. The rule was very clear. The kitchen had to be cleaned before bed, and if you did not clean it properly another week was added. I was going through a particularly hard rough patch with my oldest bonus baby Ty, because I think she wanted to go back home to her mom but did not know how to tell us this. So, I called her down to clean the kitchen and she got an attitude. Her dad and I were in the next room and we could hear her cursing, slamming cabinets and just being disrespectful in general.

I turned to him and said *"Are you going to address this behavior?"* My thoughts were that if your dad is allowing you to disrespect me in front of him, why would you listen to a word that I had to say.

In his natural dismissive tone he said *"No, you're just like her mom you go beat her ass."*

My immediate response then and my same response now was *"Hell no!"*

As a bonus parent, you follow the lead of the parent, you do not LEAD the parent in discipline. Especially in hostile situations that could escalate like the one that was unfolding before us. She felt comfortable disrespecting me because she felt totally comfortable disrespecting HIM. Just imagine the scenario, I go confront her - we are yelling and screaming at one another, she throws a punch or I slap her and a big fight has started. She calls her mom who comes to the house to confront us for touching her child (which is something I would do too) and now the snowball has grown even bigger. Not to mention, the respect has not been established between child and father or child and bonus mom. I had to step back and let that situation die down. I did not cuss her out or go off on her. If her dad was OK with her disrespecting me then that spoke volumes of how he felt about me as well.

I did not back up from that situation because I did not love my bonus baby or I saw her differently than I saw my own biological children. I backed up because I respected the fact that I was not her parent and neither of her parents required that she respected me. I had no back up. No respect for me meant that the discipline would be ineffective, so why waste my time? Discipline should come from the biological parent first and the bonus parent stands in support. As time and respect are earned, the bonus parent can venture into that discipline waters. Beware of trying to walk in hitting and punishing somebody else's child. That is not your place.

OB3's Story

If I am raising them then I am going to discipline them. That is as simple as 1+1=2. I did not walk into the relationship with a belt in my hand. I started off with having real talks with my soon-to-be wife at the time about how I felt about discipline and children. I gave her children time and space to open up to me as a person so they knew the difference between when I was playing and when I was dead ass serious. I let them watch me with my children. They saw that I was somebody worth respecting.

Discipline is 60% respect and 40% fear. You don't want to be the man that the kids hate because he is nice to mama but mean to your kids. Don't be a dumb broad and just hand your children over to a man or woman just because you love them. Everybody do not have pure intentions. You see the stories in the news about boyfriends killing babies, or stepmoms mistreating children. I am not trying to scare you. I am just being honest with you. Talk to the co-parent and the biological parent and get an understanding of what is considered acceptable. You have to give respect to get respect. Yes that means you respect the children, they are people too. If they are that out of control and you cannot deal then maybe this is the wrong relationship for you. Have a talk with the co-parent, and try to figure it out, but don't take the matter into your own hands. You will regret it if you mistreat mine. Straight up.

Chapter Ten:
Closing

Dub's Closing

We have shared with you our experiences as partners and parents over the last 20 years and exposed ourselves for a cause. The goal of this book was to force you into the uncomfortable space - that proverbial fork in the road that moves you towards forgiveness and effective co-parenting. The space that stops you from being a baby mama and transforms you into the co-parent that puts the children first in every decision, word and action that takes place after the break up for the sake of the children.

I know that it is not easy. That is why I shared so many of my true stories throughout this book. I have worn so many hats in this co-parenting team. I have been the girlfriend, the stepparent, the mistress, the wife, the mom, the ex who hated the ex, the ex who didn't want any drama and the single parent. I would scour the bookstores looking for a book that I could relate to but found nothing, so we created one. Two people who once loved each other, then hated each other, came together once again but this time to give birth to a movement instead of a child. You can move past the hurt, the betrayal and the lies to co-parent. It is not easy but it is possible. It took us 20 years to get it right with no instructions, but you have our blueprint now.

OB3's Closing

Time really does heal all wounds. I went from being a young dude married to the streets, to a young husband and father, to a complete absentee dad, to the guy sitting here writing this book hoping to help just ONE dad do better. Once you know better you do better, that is what my grandma used to tell me. Dub and I took a bunch of twists and turns to get to the place where we are today. We made a promise to keep our children first and we eventually got back to that promise. This book helped to heal a lot of wounds between Dub, the children and me. It helped our children to see us working together and gave them the confidence they needed to move beyond the divorce.

We have many more years of parenting left to complete so this won't be the last time you hear from us. Just take what we said, think on it for real, and if it makes sense use it in your life. We are not professionals by any stretch of the imagination. We are just two partners turned into parents and friends so that our babies could be the best that they could be. We did not know what you were doing, we learned by trial-and-error. You have the instructions right here in these pages. Use them.

Thank you for the ride

Dub's Thank You

OB3,

As we wrap up this project I am reflecting over the level of effort it took to coordinate and produce this honest body of work. Getting married was a bad idea, but remaining friends was the best decision we could have made. I want to thank you, for the love that you have shown to your bonus daughter. She does not have your blood but that has never stopped you for loving, protecting, teaching and caring for her. Any other man in that position would have walked away. You didn't, even after the divorce, you separated your love for her from our problems. Peanut would be proud.

Thank you for redeeming yourself during my bone marrow transplant. I did not have to worry about the children because you were right there for all of them. The pep talks, the check-ins, all of it helped me to focus on my healing and not the world crumbling around me.

Thank you for the pep talk that resurrected Dub. It saved my life.

Thank you for honoring and respecting me as the mother of your children. I know I am a basket case sometimes and that it might not have been easy after all the mistakes I've made. You were a horrible husband to me but we made some amazing, humble and happy children. We honored our 20-year promise to one another and many people cannot say that.

A very special thank you for sharing two people from your life with me. Grandpa Lou and Nicco. Grandpa Lou taught me the meaning of love as seen through God. Nicco taught me how deeply a mother's love could reach. He has stretched me in so many ways that have forced me level-up and grow. I am a better woman, mother, sister and friend because of them.

Last but certainly not least, thank you for marrying such a phenomenal and beautiful woman. She loves our children as her own and she allows and supports us in this co-parenting journey. She has turned you into the man I always knew you would be. She is the best decision you ever made. Thank you Mrs. OB3. You are very appreciated.

Open Letter to Her - Closure

Dear #1,

I would be lying if I said I didn't think about you and our failed co-parenting relationship a lot as I wrote this book. I know that you have completely moved on and life is great for you. I am so genuinely happy for you. I want to publicly apologize to you for the role I played in the destruction of your family and the degradation of our co-parenting relationship, so I am writing you this open letter.

It was not until my marriage to him was over that I realized there was nothing special about me to him. I know now that he never really chose to be with me, I was just a place to run and hide after you had finally gotten tired and let him go. I apologize for not paying attention to the signs. I apologize for ignoring my morals. Most importantly, I apologize for any hurt that I caused to you and your family. I just want you to know my love for your children is, was and always will be genuine, and was never tied to 'impressing him'. My love for them comes from my deepest space of love and remains intact. In my own way, I knew that you were never really the problem. I knew that you were not the terrible person he tried to paint you as, but I had to listen to his version of the story in order to keep myself from feeling the guilt and shame. I always understood your disdain for me and that is why I was afraid to try harder to establish a co-parenting relationship with you. I committed the ultimate taboo and I was too ashamed to face you.

I apologize for placing such harsh judgements against you for the way you handled the existence of my daughter. I also had to walk in your shoes as the wife with an outside baby by my husband's mistress during the same time, so I thought I was the ultimate authority on how you should treat the other woman and the child. I was wrong. We all handle life's curveballs differently and you handled it the best you knew how. I understand that now.

One day, Karma paid me a visit and taught me a great lesson in life. Karma shared with me that earth-shattering pain from having the man that I once loved more than life itself completely abandon, embarrass and bankrupt me in every area- emotionally, mentally, physically and financially. I know that you understand how that feels because I now understand what you had to go through. I watched you quietly glow up. I was rooting for you and praying for you by name every single day. I still pray that one day we can sit in a room together with our families in peace and forgiveness, a prayer that I know God hears and will facilitate at the perfect time for us all.

As the truth began to shine through the broken pieces of his lies I realized just how much strength it took for you to keep moving the way you did. I want you to know that it was never my mission to destroy you and I never had any ill feelings towards you. I fought him on every battle he wanted to wage against you, every time he wanted to start a petty war or fight with you just to 'show you' because I knew it was wrong. I did try my best to hold up his financial obligations to you and the girls by paying the child support payments over the years. Those came from me, not him. I did it thinking it would help me feel less guilty or that it would help you see that I was not the bad guy, but it did not. Nothing I did helped and that made me feel helpless so I stopped trying and for that I am sorry. When I found myself having to pick up the pieces of his 'storm' that tore through me and my children's lives, I knew that this was my repayment for every storm my selfish act had put you through.

I want to say thank you for sparing me the drama. You are an amazing mother. Your daughters were one of my greatest gifts and I appreciate every single second that they were part of my life. Thank you. You were an amazing wife to him, I could never fill your shoes and trust me I tried. He missed you dearly and I knew that deep down in my soul, even when I tried to ignore it. Most of all, I want to say to you again - openly and publicly - I apologize for knowingly *having a brief love affair with your husband and creating a life with him while he was still married to you. Although I was not alone in the affair - I was still wrong in my actions and I knew better. I was raised better. I am better than that. I did not think about you as a wife, mother, woman or the Queen that you are. I am deeply, sincerely and truly sorry for every single moment I acted so thoughtlessly and irresponsibly.*

You did not deserve any of it. I hope that you may find it in your heart to forgive me.

Sincerely,

Dub

OB3's Thank You

Thank you to my dope ass wife for supporting me in this project and journey.

Thank you to my children for letting me back in. I am nothing without all of you even though y'all stay digging in my pocket.

Thank you to my Grandma Millie for loving me. I survived on your love.

Thank you to my parents for showing me what not to do.

The Modern Woman's Curse
by Aset Rising

Chapter Preview: Guilt

"I can introduce you to your maker."

Jay Z, Lucifer

I can quote a Jay Z verse and a Bible verse for just about any situation in my life. But I didn't have Jay Z or a Bible verse on that rainy day in the car. The tension in the car was heavy. I sat quietly in the back seat wedged against the back door waiting for a moment to act. In the front seat, Tupac's newest song is playing in the background. I hear his raspy quick tone encouraging women to hold their heads up but the argument in the front seat drowns the positive message. I don't know how the fight started but I know that it escalated quickly and we all piled into the car to avoid bringing attention to ourselves. His anger boils over into quick jabs to her ribs at the stop sign.

"Why did you have to embarrass me in front of my boys like that?" He grunts as he threw another punch to her ribcage.

"I don't know what I did wrong. Tell me how did I embarrass you?" She whimpers trying to defend her rib cage.

"You know what the fuck you did stupid bitch!" Cat screams.

I can't take it anymore. The thoughts in my head tumble from my tongue.

"If you touch her again you will regret it Cat!" I yell over the music. This catches Mike's attention and now he's lunging toward me with all of his force. The first slap across my face leaves my ears ringing. I watch him in slow motion land another blow across my face. Instinctively I try to reach for the door. I know it's only a matter of time before he hits me again.

Emma's attention quickly moves from her abuser to mine and she reaches over the seat to restrain him.

As the car slows to a stop, I remember the blue chevy with the old man looking into the car at the chaotic scene. He mouths the words *"Are you OK?"* and his awareness gives me the courage I need. I grab the door handle and begin tumbling out of the car. Mike grabs me quickly and slams the door shut. The car speeds off and he's hurling more insults at me.

"You stupid bitch!"

"What the fuck be going through your dumb ass head?"

The fight in the front seat continues as we travel down the highway to an unknown destination. I decide to use an old trick I learned as a child to tune out the yelling and fighting. I tell myself when we come to another stop I will get out and save myself and Emma. A light rain begins to fall and the car falls silent. The faint sound of music in the background plays along with the soft cries of Emma. She doesn't understand what she has done wrong and I know she won't forgive herself for making Cat beat her again. This is the third time this weekend. I regret dating older guys in this moment. I reach over the front seat and place my hand on her back. I want her to know she is not alone in any of this. Then she say it.

"Take me home. It is over," she says quietly yet confidently.

"Bitch you can't leave me, I will run this car off of the road before you do." Cat threatens.

"Do what you have to do but I am done," Emma repeats without a hint of fear.

I am shocked and proud now thinking, *if she broke up with Cat, I can break up with Mike and this nightmare of a summer could be over.*

"Cat, noooooooooooooooooo!" I hear her screaming!

In seconds, we've gone from cruising down the highway to going full speed into the concrete barrier on the exit ramp. Our bodies fly forward and there is a loud thump. The sound of metal and the smell of smoke fills my nostrils before I pass out briefly. When I come to Mike is pulling me from the car. It's flipped on its side. Cat is standing on the side of the road pacing, screaming and crying. I look around for Emma, knowing she is afraid and needing me but she is nowhere to be found.

"Where is Emma?" I whisper.

Silence.

"Where is Emma??!?!" I yell.

"She is still in the car, I can't get her out!" Cat sobs as I pounds him with my small, weak fists.

"Do something!" Mike yells as cars slow down to help us.

I sit on the side of the freeway with the sound of cars zooming by and I wail. The next few hours play out like a scene in a tragic movie. We watch in horror as the jaws of life pry open the hood to get Emma out of the car.

Silently, we sit in the emergency room waiting for the doctors to tell us that she was going to be OK. Her dad arrives, he is disheveled and afraid. His anger leads him straight to Cat's throat. He doesn't land a punch, His grief has rendered him helpless. He questions me again and again, but words do not form.

No. I don't know what we were thinking.

No. I have no idea how upset he must feel.

No. I don't know what made us sneak off and betray our parents' trust like that.

I sit there, silently crying and praying that my friend's life will be spared.

Hours later the doctors finally walk into the waiting room and I know immediately.

"I'm sorry...but", the doctor began. All of the oxygen in the room disappears and is replaced with raw pain as I listen to the doctor recount how he tried to save Emma's life, in vain. The only thing that stops my tears is watching the police officers approach Cat and place him in handcuffs. He does not resist. He is too tired from crying and pleading with God. Mike slips out of a side door before his friend is arrested.

Fourteen is too young to comprehend death.

A new friend was introduced to me in the weeks following the death of Emma. She was very subtle and quiet, yet her presence was very powerful. Guilt was her name. She reassured my thoughts day and night. Yes, it was absolutely my fault that she was dead. Yes, I could have done more to stop it. Yes, I should have tried harder to get help. Yes, this was my fault. Guilt and I spent a lot of time with each other in those early days. The worst thing about having such a reassuring friend with me at all times is that the guilt fueled me to check out of life. Things that I once found enjoyable, such as the cool breeze in the early morning or a good song on the radio, suddenly had no meaning to me. I spent a lot of time reading books and escaping into the imaginary world of fiction novels. I went from being a vibrant and social teenager to a quiet introspective miniature adult. Guilt would wake me up in the middle of the night to talk about what happened. I would listen to her soothing voice as she replayed the events. A strange thing began to happen to me during these late night conversations. Guilt's voice slowly transformed from my voice to Emma's voice. Others would think I was crazy if I told them that, so I did not. I was comforted by the fact that she was there and talking to me again. Even if it was just to agree with my guilt it eased my mourning and allowed me to feel connected to her again. I began to look forward to those late night conversations with Guilt narrated by Emma.

Masks are effective tools to hide your pain. Several weeks following her death, I put on my first mask. I resumed my normal life activities with a bounce in my step and a smile on my face. Bubbly and full of life and knock-knock jokes, I slowly began to reassure everyone around me that the whole situation was behind me and I was ready to move forward. I enjoyed riding public transportation because it allowed me to people watch. Fascinated by the lives of others, I would single out a person on the bus and create an entire life for them. The lady with the long red nails was a secretary at a big firm downtown. I imagined her eating her lunch at the desk and taking phone calls as she painted her nails. The older gentleman reading the newspaper was a proud grandfather that saved tootsie rolls in his pockets for the visits with his grandchildren. I glanced around, bored with my current imaginary lives, to find another younger person to serve as my creative muse. I scanned the bus and my heart stopped.

Mike. He was standing less than three feet away and staring directly at me. All contact was severed on that day in the emergency room. Now, he was back in my presence looking to me as if years had passed. His appearance was jarring although, in most ways, the same. Big baggy jeans barely fit his waist. His huge basketball jersey draped his thin frame. His long face was accented with a large diamond earring hanging from his tiny earlobe. He wore several large flat herringbone necklaces of different lengths. He had two beepers clamped to his side, one red and one black. His dopeman Nikes were crisp and fresh out of a shoe box. His brown eyes twinkled and a small smile curled on the edge of his lip. I looked around for the nearest exit and felt imprisoned because he was inches away from the door. I pulled the bell to get off the bus. I had no idea where I was in the city but I knew I had to get off of that bus and away from my past.

The bus screeched to a halt and all of the passengers jerked forward. I pushed past the lady with the red nails and the grandpa reading a paper and jumped down the stairs to freedom. My lungs filled with the fresh air and the sun hit my skin to remind me that I was no longer confined to a space with him. There was a corner store across the street and I instinctively ran towards the store oblivious of the oncoming traffic. Horns blared as my ears pounded. The sound of a bell ringing as I entered the store calmed me. I was safe. I'd made it away. I didn't need anything in the store, but I walked through each aisle pretending to look for something. The owner, an older Asian lady, trailed me as I did. I didn't care. Her presence was comforting.

The bell rang again. Someone walked into the store. Fear paralyzed me as I waited to see who'd walked in. It was a group of kids laughing and joking looking for the sour pickles. I exhaled and settled on a bag of chips and a soda. As I walked to the front of the store to pay I began to relax and a smile spread across my face. I told myself I was being silly. The older Asian lady told me my total and as I searched for my purse to pay I realized that I'd dropped it on the bus. My cash, bus transfer, lip gloss and keys were all in that purse and panic washed over me. I turned to walk away and there he was again.

"You left this." Mike said, his voice, familiar and even. He held my Dooney & Bourke purse with his pinky finger extended towards me.

"Thank you." I replied as I yanked my purse from his grip.

I paid for my items and headed for the door. This time I did not run. I walked calmly and slowly towards the exit and paused to feel the sun on my skin. He was right behind me asking me something but I didn't hear him. My thoughts were consumed with Guilt, my familiar friend. I should not be able to walk this earth and feel this sun when my friend's life was cut short so tragically.

"Slow down. I just want to talk to you," he pleaded.

"*Mike, there is nothing to talk about. If you do not leave me alone I will scream,*" I hissed.

"*I am sorry about Emma!*" He yelled.

I stopped in my tracks, "*Never say her name to me again.*" I said as I walked towards him in anger.

"*Never speak her name to anyone again. You don't have the right!*" My anger swelled in my chest and the weeks of isolation and guilt fueled my righteous indignation. I felt no fear, only anger and I began to pummel his chest with my fists.

"*I am so sorry.*" He repeated. This time it was soft and heart felt. He allowed my fists to connect to his chest over and over again until the tears began to spill from my eyes and his. Mike pulled me in close to his chest and held my head as I sobbed. The tears were hot and salty as they mixed with snot. The emotion was so overwhelming to me because it had been bottled up. I was sickened by the fact that I was being comforted by a man who had caused my grief, yet I was strangely relieved. There are billions of people on this earth and only two other people could understand the crushing emotion that I was swimming in at that moment.

After a few moments, the tears began to slow and I yanked away from him.

"Leave me alone. I am fine." I mumbled. I said it more to convince myself. Curiosity struck me and I wanted to know what had happened to him.

"Where is cat? Why did you leave that day?" I questioned.

"Cat is in jail. He had no bail. They charging him with vehicular manslaughter. I had to leave, I had warrants and I had the package on me I could not be arrested." He explained.

"She's gone. Life is never going to be the same."

He was quiet for a few moments before he said, "I'm here though. You're not in this alone." Suddenly his abusive ways took a backseat to my grief. I needed him.

"...if I prepare a place for you, I will come back and take you to be with me that you may also be where I am."

John 14:3

Aset's Bio

Aset is Carmela's daughter. She is a devoted sister, ride-or-die friend and the happily divorced mother of five children. She has been asked how she has raised such happy, healthy and thriving children. Aset's tribe has watched her go through a terminal illness, rounds of chemo and a bone marrow transplant, two terrible marriages, birthing and caring for babies, while pursuing her higher education, maintaining a steady career and traveling the world. You can add author to that list, now. What started out as a joke has become Aset's first book co-authored with her ex-husband, co-parent and good friend, OB3. Aset's mission is to empower women and let them know that their power lies within and imperfect is the new perfect.

OB3's Bio

OB3 didn't want children, his childhood left him scarred and skeptical. But today he is the proud and dedicated father of six beautiful children. He went from being married to the streets to being the happily and honorable husband of his beautiful wife. In his no holds barred style, he gives you the facts about how he grew from a boy into a man and a father. His tone is as serious as his topic and as real and raw as the life he's lived. He has become a man who loves his family more than anything. He provides an example to all his readers of how to step up to the plate, do the hard work to make things right and handle your responsibility as a parent. Honoring a promise he made over 20 years ago, he has remained committed to caring for his children and always keeping them first. OB3's legacy remains his top priority. This is his first book.

The Exes' Bio

Aset Rising and OB3 met in high school and were married with children when most people their age were in college and living life. They were married for over ten years and have been friends for almost twenty years. Their marriage faced affairs, poverty, lack of family support, dreams deferred, death and much more. The book, Instructions Not Given was their idea. It was a joke OB3 and Aset Rising made out of the constant suggestion of friends and relatives that their lives were like a soap opera. These two people rose from the hurt they caused one another and turned their methods of coping into a book that honors a twenty year old promise made to one another to keep the children first.

www.ingramcontent.com/pod-product-compliance
Lightning Source LLC
Chambersburg PA
CBHW070928030426
42336CB00014BA/2585